From the Barrel to the Bar

For my dad

&,

for my three beautiful, perfect children. I love you so very much.

Contents

Acknowledgements

I wish to offer my grateful thanks to all those who have encouraged and supported me in my endeavours. I also thank the people who are no longer with us, like my grandmother. She only ever made positive comments towards me and about me. It is thanks to the likes of her that I have kept a positive mindset during the most difficult of times.

I would also like to thank the ones who didn't support me, who had nothing other than negative comments about my goals. They have supported me more than they could ever realise, as it is thanks to them that I got the extra push that I needed. It is thanks to the negative comments that kept me going when I thought that I couldn't do it. I would recall the comments about my goals, and even comments about my written grammar. Those negative comments helped me get through it all, thank you.

I thank me, I thank me for believing in me, for never giving up on me, and for fighting for me during so many difficult times. I thank me for being strong and resilient, battling for my children and setting the correct example before them. I thank me for working hard and providing for my children. I thank me for fighting to keep the home, a family home that my children are familiar with, and that one day adds to their future inheritance. I thank Merseyside police, particularly their armed response team. It was thanks to them that the area was cleared at speed and made safe for the medics to go in and attend to me.

Acknowledgements

5

I thank the armed police officer who sat at my bed side, he didn't need to talk, but he did. I had no one at that moment, so it was nice to hear a friendly voice. I thank the surgeons and the NHS who all saved me that terrible New Years eve night. It is thanks to them that I have both legs. I thank the physio who spent so much time with me, which helped me gain strength in my leg and assisted in my full recovery.

I finally thank God for always being at my side, for never giving up on me. I thank the lord for giving me a second chance of life, and I hope that I made him proud and continue to make him proud.

'Once he was lost, but now he is found!'

Prologue

This book is a work of non-fiction and is based on actual events. The names have been kept hidden and changed to protect identities. I have also changed some locations in the Cheshire area to also protect identities. I gained advice from Merseyside police who advised me to remove information from my first draft, as it contained discussions I had with Merseyside CID where evidence was discussed. I was reminded that there is still an attempted murder charge outstanding. The story describes my personal experiences in life as a youngster growing up in a rough area of Huyton, Liverpool. The city of Liverpool is in the North West of England and known to many due to the amount of success that the city has produced. The city is known for producing many sports stars, musicians, artists, playwriters, actors. The list is endless and far too many to mention. I was very fortunate as a youngster to train with a few of the boxing stars, such as Paul Hoko, Alex Moon and others. My experience growing up was typical in the Huyton area. You would have to learn how to fight at speed. You would also have to learn how to lose, as you would be guaranteed to lose a few fights. You needed to learn how to walk with your head held high and avoid bullying by anyone that you lost to. The book will highlight the issues I encountered at school due to many behaviour issues I possessed. My story leads up to one fatal night, where I was shot three times. I will describe what I went through during and after the incident.

Prologue

I will also describe the troubles I experienced when getting divorced and having to fight for access to my children. I will highlight how I didn't appear to care when it came to consequences for any wrongful acts I committed. I will describe some incidents that may even appear funny, but when looking back, a lot of the incidents could have gone horribly wrong. The main aim of this book is to highlight the importance of time, and to send a message to youngsters that there is nothing tough or good about being shot at or hanging out with tough guys. I want my story to promote academic achievements, and for youngsters in the likes of Huyton to realise that they have a great opportunity in making a success for themselves, but it must start at school. If they can make a success at school, then they are steps ahead of the game. I want people to read my story and think about how much time I have wasted, how academic talent has been wasted too, as I was always capable, but didn't act until well into my 40s. The time for academic success is when one is young, get it all out the way as quickly as possible, and start planning for a career. There are far too many idiots on the likes of social media, as good as promoting the gangster life, making it sound like a good thing. They are losers and idiots, and they aren't tough, far from it. The real tough men are the ones who go to work and bring home a pay cheque for their partners and who support their children. I want my story to send out a positive message and hopefully my description of my academic success sends out the right message.

Chapter One

The most comfortable state

I always assumed one would be in tremendous pain if suffering from a gunshot wound, and that you would be screaming in agony. When we watch movies, we create a perception of what it would be like. I never thought I would be able to one day describe the true feelings of what it is *really* like. As the pub was in a state of panic, I lay completely relaxed and in a calm state of mind watching everyone running around in slow motion. I couldn't hear the screaming, but I could see that many were screaming with panic etched on their faces. The first bullet entered my stomach and exited my back, approximately six inches above the waistline on my left side. The first bullet hit no major organs and was a clean hit. The second bullet caused the most damage. It entered my right buttock, smashing its way through my hip bone and bouncing around my right leg causing damage to my hip and femur. There was a two-inch gap in my femur caused from the bullet laced in Teflon. They soak bullets in Teflon to cause as much damage as possible. Teflon is what is applied to non-stick frying pans, and it causes the bullets to bounce from whatever it hits, bouncing around like a pinball. The second bullet rested on the femoral artery, and this is what could've killed me. If that artery started bleeding, I was as good as done for. The third bullet entered my left foot and travelled up my leg towards the knee.

I thought I wet myself at first. I reached around and without knowing I placed my four fingers into the exit wound. I then realised I had not wet myself; it was blood spilling out of my body. The hole at the rear was large, around the size of a ping pong ball. The skin was closing, but I could still feel the blood spilling out, so I looked around for something to hold against the hole. I spotted a beer mat on the floor and pressed it against my back to stop the blood pouring. I knew I was dying, as I could feel that I was slipping away. Suddenly, there was a smack across my face and a middle-aged blonde female was leaning over me, she was shouting, 'don't go to sleep love, stay awake'. I started to panic and in silence I prayed for help. Two males stood by laughing, one stated in a thick Liverpool accent, 'he's goosed him La, well dying, he is shot up to fuck'. Those horrifying words caused panic inside me, but my body had no ability to move. I was suffering in silence; it was like I was screaming from inside a locked room. I needed my mind to grab hold of a nice thought or memory to prevent the panic that was happening inside me, and to take my mind off the realisation that I was dying. I pictured my mum worried, knowing she would be upset if she saw me lying on the floor in this state. I started to smile at the thought of her shouting at me, 'Why are you there in that rough pub, we have worked so hard to live in a nice place, why are aren't you at home with us?' I suddenly felt another smack on my face from the blonde who was again leaning over me shouting, 'don't you die on me love, the ambulance will be here any minute'. I started to drift off into an even more relaxed state. I started to picture my great grandmother on my mother's side. I have no idea why she popped into my mind, but she was as clear as day standing in front of me.

She was holding me in her arms with my grandmother's black, back garden gate in the background. I was approximately three years old at the time as she held me. I suddenly felt a warmth run over me, it was a feeling of love, as though someone was caring for me. I was starting to feel that everything would be okay and so I grabbed hold of the image of my great grandmother, as it provided me with a sense of security and love. My body started to feel like jelly, it was as though I was floating in a swimming pool. I was totally relaxed, but the jelly feeling wasn't nice. I continued to watch the people run with fear, knocking chairs and tables over as they ran. A few jumped over the bar, hiding. I kept picturing men walking into the pub wearing balaclavas, then standing over me with guns, firing until I was dead. My heart was beating fast, and as I started to go into panic, my great grandmother would appear again and bring back a feeling of comfort, keeping me calm. I then heard the blonde female say out loud, 'fucking hell, there is blood pissing out of him everywhere, where the fuck is the ambulance?', and just as she shouted, there was a sudden feeling of terror amongst the people in the pub. Then, a loud bang, as multiple armed police officers dressed in black came bursting into the pub. 'Police, are you armed? Are you fucking armed lad?' and then another gun pointed directly at my face, 'Police, you any guns on ya lad?' For a moment I thought I was part of a movie, such as Platoon. I had no real fear as the police had guns in my face. I was way past fear, I was dying and accepting my fate. A few moments passed, and I noticed that I had several paramedics around me. I could overhear them talking, commenting on how much I was bleeding. I was then carried out on a stretcher to an ambulance.

There was a helicopter hovering low with a large spotlight. It was starting to resemble a war movie even more so at this point. I briefly saw many people surrounding the pub car park as I was carried past them. I heard police officers swearing and shouting aggressively for people to get away and to stay behind the line. I was put into an ambulance and felt the acceleration and urgency in getting me to the hospital. I asked the paramedic if I was dying, I told him to tell my mum, dad, sister, and brother that I love them, and that I am sorry. He asked me, 'sorry for what?' I replied, 'I don't know, as I have not done anything'. The paramedic laughed for a moment. He asked me what went on. I replied, 'I was doing the door, and it was only my fourth time. The other doormen were mates I knew from my boxing club. I am only 5ft 10, and am not big enough to do the door, I was only doing it as we would go straight out to town afterwards, and it was a way of getting free drinks and £60 for town was all, I am not involved in any of that what's gone on tonight, I am not into drugs and have never even smoked.' He told me to calm down, and so I did. I lay there and started to relax once more. Suddenly I felt my face being smacked and my top ripped open. The van came to a stop, and I felt cold on my chest. I was being jerked forwards and backwards. I can't remember much after that, other than waking up at a hospital table with approximately five nurses and doctors surrounding me. The nurse leaned over me and told me that the next procedure would not be pleasant. I looked around and there were lots of wires and tubes hanging from me and going into me too. One of them was a large blood bag, this caused me worry. The next thing I saw was a large steel-looking rod. It was like a giant-sized thick steel pencil, around twenty inches long. The nurse lubricated it and then started to place it in the entry wound, and with her other hand she placed two fingers into the exit wound.

She told me they needed to check if the two holes were connected. As I lay on the table, surrounded by nurses and doctors poking and prodding me, I looked up and I saw my parents. My mother started crying and shouting at me, 'why are you out in that pub and in a rough area like that? We have worked so hard to live in a nice place, why aren't you at home with us?' I looked at my father's face, it was a face of disappointment. This would cause me more upset than any amount of shouting. My parents were removed by the nurses, and as I looked up, a police officer who was standing near the rear of the bed pointed at my shoe. He pointed to my left sole, saying that there was a hole, and blood is dripping from it. The doctor said out loud to the nurse beside me, 'I think there is a fourth wound'. The doctor explained to me that they were working out how many times I have been shot, and for me to not worry as my signs were stable. I then felt nurses and doctors poking and prodding every inch of my body. I sensed that they were concerned about my right leg and hip area. The doctor explained that the femur was badly damaged and broken but the bleeding was under control. However, he said it may get worse during surgery, and as a result I could lose my leg, as it may be the only way to stop the bleeding. He explained to me that the bullet may be lodged in the femoral artery area, and it is a concern. Little did the doctors know at that stage that the bullet was indeed, lodged in the femoral artery area. I started to cry inside, and instantly pictured myself on one leg, unable to play football with my brother. I thought that my life would be over. It was a horrendous feeling of fear rushing through me. The doctor held my hand and told me not to worry and that I was in safe hands. I asked him how he could see the bullets inside me.

He asked me to stay calm and to not worry. I was taken to a secret ward at the hospital, where armed police officers were sat beside my bed. I immediately looked at the guns and asked, 'is someone coming to get me?' He replied, 'I hope not, but I am here just in case'. The officer was dressed all in black. However, the other police officer was dressed in a smart suit, and he also too had a gun, but I may have been mistaken. He leaned over me saying, 'big mistake if anyone comes after you in here lad, so don't worry, we are here'. I sensed that this officer in a suit was a real tough individual and not to be messed with as he must have been around 6ft 5 and was of large build. I lay back into the pillow, but I was far too concerned and worried about losing my leg to relax fully, so I asked the officer to pass me the blue bible that was beside my bed. I turned to the story of the lost son. I read the first page and started to cry, as I felt I was a failure. The officer asked me if I was okay. I asked him how long he had been an armed officer, he replied that this was his first evening. He appeared young in the face, and worried, with slight fear. I was instantly thinking that if he is worried whilst having a large gun, then how the hell should I be feeling?

'Thank you, Lord, thank you for giving me a second chance. I promise to improve, and I always do the best I can with achieving and setting the correct example.'

The Lost Son.

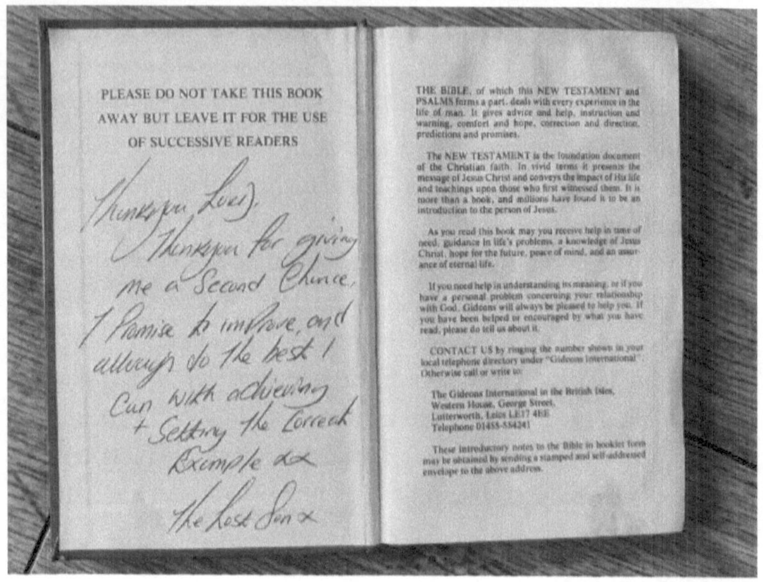

The very book that helped me at hosptial

I started to chat with the officer as though he had been a friend of mine for many years. He was asking me how I ended up in this mess. I told him I started boxing age eight and became friends with many people over the years. We all had nothing to do with what was going on, and that we were just looking forward to a night on the town after doing the door.

I then heard a well-spoken voice ask me how I was and a middle-aged male with a dickie bow stood over me touching my feet and legs. He couldn't see my stomach, as that was all wrapped up to stop the bleeding, and there were tubes inside me too. He got out a pencil of some kind and started to draw on my body. He was drawing on my left leg. I stated, 'you do know that it is my right leg which is the bad one?' He started to laugh and then began wetting his fingertips, rubbing out the drawings on my left leg. He went onto to say, 'don't worry, we would have noticed which leg it was in theatre'. I began to panic at the thought that I had a real nutcase for a surgeon, and that the odds massively increased with losing my leg due to who was operating on it. The surgeon walked away and left me alone worrying, whilst the police officer started to laugh, but I didn't find it amusing. A few short moments passed, and the surgeon appeared once more, saying to me, 'yes, the left leg is also bad, just so you know, as a bullet has travelled up towards the knee area.' The police officer didn't laugh this time, as he must have realised just how bad of a state I was in, but little did he know that I needed to hear laughing at that moment, as laughing made me feel for a short moment that all was okay. I started to think about where my life went wrong, I was reminding myself that I had a mortgage at age twenty-one, still young, and it was still only a couple of years from first getting that mortgage. Each time I attempted to take my mind off the thought of losing my leg, something would pop into my mind, such as a picture of myself with only one leg. A nurse appeared in front of me, messing with the tubes, and stated that she needed to turn something up. She asked me if I was okay, and I replied that I was worried about losing my leg. She sat beside me and informed me that there are many mechanical devices to help and assist with walking now.

The nurse then stated, 'making it out alive is the first concern you should have'. She then walked away. I was left wondering whether I would live or not, also shocked, and surprised that she said such a thing. I said out loud to the officer, 'I can't believe she just said that'. The officer smiled and replied, 'I was shocked at that too.' I needed to relax somehow, as the panic was getting too much. I started to try and think of nice thoughts. I somehow got back to thinking where it all went wrong and how I ended up in this state. I always had a sharp memory which enabled me to think back to pivotal memories of my early years. This process allowed me to go through the years and see why I ended up lying here wondering whether I may die or not.

Scare from surgery

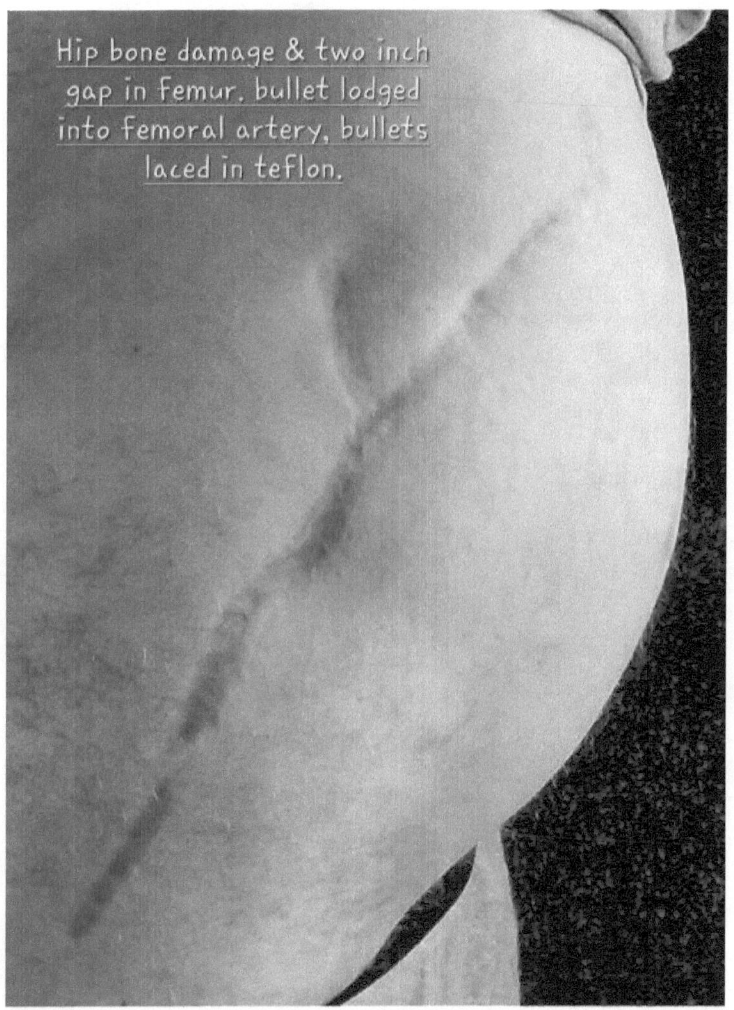

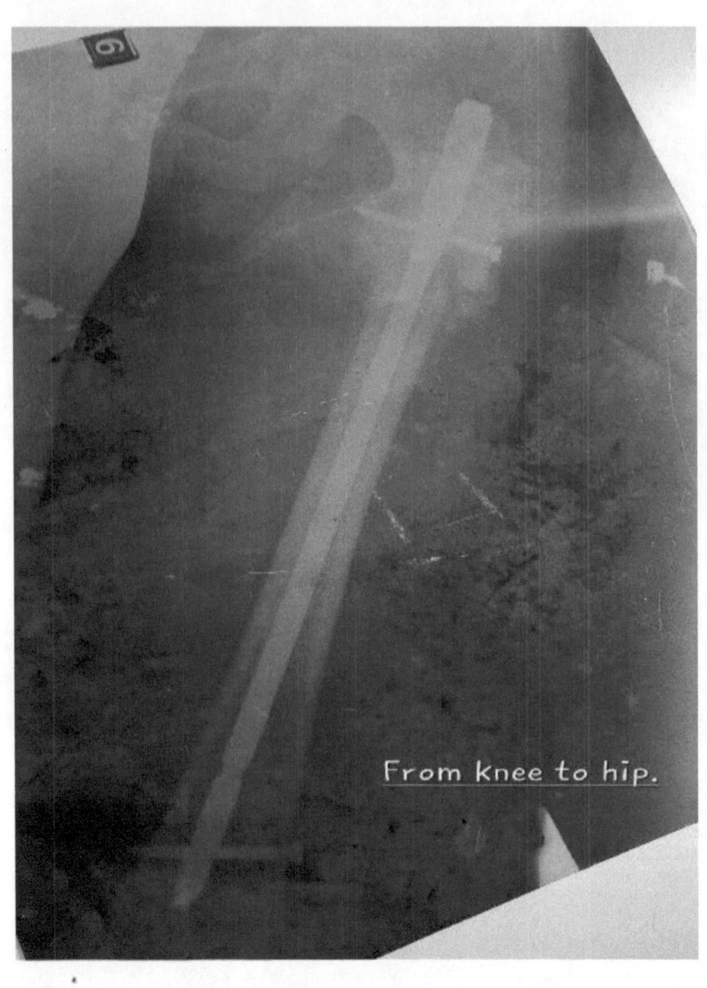

The titanium rod that is the full length of my femur

*The bullet wound scare at the base of my foot, and
the entry and exit wound to my stomach area*

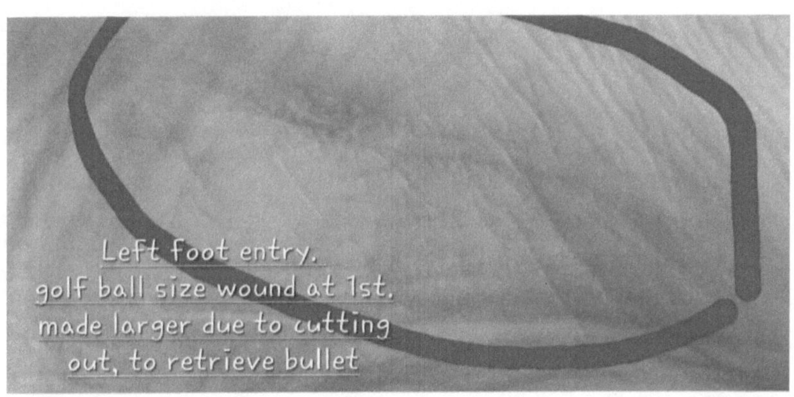

Chapter Two

The early years

I guess it all began in Bruton Road, Huyton, Liverpool, as this is where I was born. My parents were very young when having me. My mother was sixteen and my dad seventeen. It was a massive no, no back then to have a child out of wedlock. My grandparents on my mother's side were very traditional. My mother was heavily pregnant during her marriage, and I can't begin to imagine the concern all grandparents must have had with having a child who was dealing with a pregnancy at such a young age. I am aware that many friends and family during that time had little faith in my parents making it, but my parents proved everyone wrong. I personally believe it was love that was the secret of their success.

My upbringing was tough, and there was lots of chastising. I was out of control, even from a very young age. I was cock of the infants, cock meaning the toughest in the school. I would have only been around age seven or eight at the time, but I still remember getting into trouble for fighting. I would often have my shoes removed due to kicking others, and I also remember receiving the cane at age eight. I remember it clearly, as it was my last year at Stockbridge Infants. I found out that the Head needed my parents' permission, and he got it. I hated my mother for providing permission. I still, even today have a very small scar where the cane hit my palm. Blood was drawn that day, and I held my hand in pain, trying to hold back the tears so the head would not know he hurt me. I looked down and spotted blood and shouted out towards him. I cannot remember what I shouted, and I dread to think. It was obvious I was going to be a handful. When I was just age five, I left my grandmother's house without permission wearing her shoes and got onto a bus to Liverpool. I got off the bus and wandered to the waterfront, ending up sitting on a bench admiring the view of the Mersey. My parents had half of the Liverpool Police Force out looking for me. I was found and came home in a police car whilst wearing a police officer's hat. My grandparents on my mother's side also lived in Bruton Road, they lived at the top end. My mum's eldest sister lived at the bottom end of Bruton Road. The family was large and very close. My grandparents had a total of nine children, they were very respected in the area, as they were lovely people. My grandfather was known as Basher to the few, he was a tough hard-working man. He was a perfect role model for me, as he was a good father, grandfather, and husband. He had worked hard all his life and when he retired, he continued to work regularly in the garden. He loved painting too, and in his shed, there would be many painted pictures hanging. I am aware he worked selling ice creams in the Isle of Man when he was young, but his main career was working over 30 years on the docks at Liverpool. The docks are where he got the name, Basher, his father was also known as Basher apparently. I heard his father got the name when fighting with a police officer. I can still remember the day he took me to Liverpool docks; I would have only been around six years old at the time.

This picture was taken in a photo booth at Liverpool, during the day out at the docks.

My grandmother was beyond perfect. I miss her daily, and always will. During the war she made parachutes I believe. I am aware she also made a name for herself as a Seamstress. She had customers throughout Huyton who would visit her home with dress designs, they were mostly wedding dresses. I would often see people at my grandmothers' collecting dresses that she had made.

I have happy memories of Bruton Road, we moved when I would have been age eight, but I still remember walking up to my grandmothers at Christmas whilst it was snowing. It was a great time of my life; I was very loved by the family and guess that was because I was one of the first grandchildren. My mums' sisters were all lovely. I would often be found in one of my auntie's rooms, mostly playing on my uncle's Commodore 64, or asking my favourite auntie about Elvis. I miss those days so very much.

We moved from Bruton Road and into Gentwood Road, it was only around three miles away and still in Huyton. I would still visit my grandmother daily, and regularly sat up with my Granddad watching the same movies repeatedly. He must have watched First Blood a thousand times. He would often have me polishing his shoes and we would spend hours cleaning them and once I finished, he would inspect them, providing me with instructions if the shine wasn't to his satisfaction. Everything was better during this period of my life. Bonfire night would include a huge fire, and many surrounding neighbours would all join in. We would play duck apple, this involved trying to bite an apple out of a bowl of water and biting apples that hung from string. My aunties would play Kerby with me, Kerby is a game where you throw a ball and try to hit the curb side next to the road. I now realise how fortunate I was to have had this kind of upbringing, as you very rarely see children playing ball games in the road these days. I have many fond memories of being a child visiting my grandmothers, I loved being around the family. I once sat at the rear of my uncle's motorbike scooter as he drove me around Hillside, Hillside being the road that ran parallel with Bruton Road. I loved all my uncles. My uncle with the motorbike was probably the one I looked up to the most, and he most likely didn't know that.

He once got me a massive picture of a sports car from work. I can still remember him taking it out of the boot of his car. Hillside had a notorious name back then, and still does now. Every Friday and Saturday without fail there would be a stolen car taking chase from the police cars. Sometimes they would set the car on fire and smash it up on the Hillside oller. The Oller was like a massive roundabout, and many youths would have a fire on it every weekend, standing around and waiting to watch the stolen cars pass by. I once watched a horror movie at my grandmother's house, The Lost Boys and I remember my uncle saying to me, 'don't look up whilst you're peddling home tonight'. I peddled as fast as I could to get home that evening. It was always fun and games at my grandmothers and I would, at times, enjoy winding my uncles and aunties up. Looking back, I can see how I must have been extremely annoying at times.

It was always like a mini event when my grandmother made a pot of tea. Everyone would sit around the table and talk. There would always be cake and sandwiches waiting. I still picture those days, and it can be upsetting looking back, as I miss those days so much, especially being around the family. When my grandfather passed it was very upsetting as he suffered from dementia. It is only now looking back that I realise how everyone wanted what was best for him. I look back in regret, as I bad mouthed a few people which shames me to this day. The issue growing up in a large family is that you grow up in an environment that would involve many people talking about each other. This had an influence on me growing up. Overall, the family, including cousins were close. There are a lot of cousins, as everyone seemed to have had a minimum of three children. Looking back, I have no idea how everyone managed to fit into my grandmother's small house.

My favourite cousins lived in Leigh, one was in the army and even today he still messages me to see how I am, and I talk to the other cousin almost daily. I have always looked up to the one who joined the army, I remember us going to a local park with his air rifle. I would love visiting Leigh where these two cousins lived, as it was an escape for me. My uncle and auntie are both very loving, and caring people. I still feel at home when visiting them today. When I visited my auntie recently, she told me a little memory she had where my cousin wanted to give me a Star Wars figure. He told my auntie he wanted to give me it, but apparently, I replied that I wanted them all. I have nothing but lovely memories being at my aunties, I am still very close to them and my cousins. I still laugh with my other cousin about how I use to be cheeky to her friends. I value my friendship and the closeness that I have with these cousins very much.

When we moved to Gentwood Road, it would involve me having to attend a new school. I attended Park View Juniors, and I had no friends for the first few months. I would sit next to a large chestnut tree daily on my own, daydreaming. My sister attended the infants at Park View and I would watch her play, making sure she was okay. You could never miss my sister at that age, as you could see her long, curly hair from a mile away. It didn't take long for me to gain my confidence and once I did, I began to misbehave. I was involved in several fights at Parkview, I remember losing one fight, and this caused me embarrassment, which turned into anger. I would attend school frustrated for the following few weeks and disrupt the class. I was put onto a report book, this involved having to hand in the report book to each teacher and they would write how I behaved that day. Mr. Dixon came up with the idea, he was a brilliant teacher, and he cared very much about all the pupils, even the badly behaved ones like me. Mr. Adams was the head, and it wasn't long before I received the cane again. Due to this I developed a huge grudge with the head of the school. I once climbed onto the school roof and as Mr. Adams shouted for me to get down, I put two fingers up to him. My parents were at a loss what to do with me. The school arranged a meeting with my parents and decided to refer me to a child psychologist. I still remember that visit, it was to a small clinic in Liverpool. I was picturing all kinds during the morning of the assessment. I pictured them putting wires in my head and electric shock treatment. I had no idea how they would assess me. To my relief they got me to complete puzzles, math, and reading out loud. The report was completed and for some reason, it made my mother proud, as it stated that I was highly intelligent. It explained that the issues were down to me having a pre-conceived idea what the lessons were about before others, and then becoming bored. I always got the point that was trying to be made by the teachers at speed. I did make a couple of good friends whilst at ParkView school. They both lived at Twig Lane, which was just around the corner from where I lived at Gentwood. Even today I have an urge to try and contact them to see how they are doing. I was once working at my father's store many years after I left Park View, and a lady approached me telling me that she's the mother of my friend from Park View who lived at Twig Lane, and that she remembered me. There weren't many happy memories at ParkView Junior School, as I didn't really feel at home there. I do remember an older boy who was two years above me picking on me. He appeared jealous, I assumed he was jealous because I attended a boxing club. I once boxed at St Aloysius club, a club that was based just across the road from my school. One evening, children at Park View climbed the walls and peered through the window to watch me fight. I won that night and knocked down an experienced amateur several times. I walked into school the next day feeling proud. However, this older boy walked straight up to me and punched me in the face. I ran home upset and my mother was extremely angry, she made me tell her where he lived. My mother knocked on the door and threatened the boy's mother. He didn't come near me after that. My mother had no fear and would often lose control. There was a school holiday trip coming up in my 2nd to last year at Park View. There were discussions if I was to be allowed to go, thankfully, after several meetings, it was finally decided that I was allowed to go onto the school holiday trip to the Isle of Man. I had to always walk alongside teachers was just one of the many conditions placed on me.

I got together with four of my friends one evening and we formed a gang called, 'Degsy's midnight runners.' We would run around the hotel late at night. I did get into trouble one evening, as an older girl invited me into her room, I sneaked in, but a teacher heard me giggling, and I had to hide under the girl's bed quickly. The teacher came in looking to see if anyone else was in the room. The teacher found me hiding under the bed and dragged me out by my ear. During this time, my father worked as a security guard at Liverpool fruit market. I went to work with my dad a few times and would sit with him whilst he worked nights. I remember his friend, Tommy. They both had Ford Cortina cars and would often race around the fruit market late at night. I would often have to listen to my dad providing me with advice on life as we drove to and from the fruit market. He would often talk about other men and tell me to watch how they acted. My dad was great at weighing people up, he could sense sly people a mile away. He appeared to have a gift at reading people and knowing their true colours at speed.

My dad was a hard worker, he worked all his life from a young age; he was a very liked man. You would struggle to find anyone who would bad mouth my dad. He would have us going door to door selling potatoes, fruit, and veg. I would walk for hours knocking door to door from the age of seven. My dad had so many business ideas. Once, we even did scrap iron. I would help my dad shout for scrap iron and help him load anything we found onto the van. My uncle would come with us, as he worked for my dad during a few of these business adventures. I enjoyed the experience very much.

My dad tried out many of his business ideas, and I would help him with each one. My dad ended up working at Ian Skelly's car show room as a car salesman. He once won salesmen of the year, and I remember him bringing home a brochure where we could pick an item from it. My mum chose a cutlery set, which arrived in a fancy wooden box. The best memory I have of my dad working at Skelly's was during a time it was snowing on my way to school. I was waiting at the bus stop for the bus to school with my mate and a few other people from my school. My dad suddenly pulled a large handbrake skid in a fancy, red, scirocco sports car with red matching seats. It was an amazing sight to watch as he slid it across the snow towards the bus stop. He gave me and my mate, John, a lift to school. He was sliding in and out of traffic, and for the rest of the day I was the talk of the school, as everyone was saying how cool my dad was. My dad finally left Skelly's and started work at the Prudential. The Pru, as he named it, was an insurance company. He didn't seem happy in his role, and it wasn't long before he left and bought his first shop. This is a memory I remember clearly as we went to Huyton village and attended Barclays bank where my dad withdrew £6,000 cash. It looked like a million pounds.

He placed the money into my inside leather coat pocket, as he thought that no one would think a young 13-year-old boy would be carrying that amount of money. We walked fast to my dad's car and straight to the shop. My dad handed his money over, whilst several large men stood by to make sure that the exchange went smoothly. My mum briefly worked in an office at Whiston, but she soon left to join my dad at the shop. I still remember the shop being empty and it was a very worrying time wondering if they would turn it into a successful business.

My parents were very determined young adults, and it was no shock that they would go on to build a successful business owning several grocery stores. My parents sold out in the end to Tesco and today the main shop is a large Tesco Express. I often look back at how hard my parents worked during those years. They would miss out on holidays, as they would invest constantly in the shops. My dad always wanted me to work in the shops, and I did. However, I always ended up arguing with my mum which resulted in me walking out and making my way to my grandmothers, as Bruton Road was just a few miles away from my dad's shops. My mother would verbally attack me at times for no reason whatsoever. It wasn't nice and affected my personality at times growing up. My sister was handed a florist to run, that my dad purchased, she also had issues when working for my parents. I wasn't allowed to attend the senior school that my friends at Park view were going to, as my parents thought that by taking me to a school out of the area where I knew no one would help me progress in my studies, but it was not long before I gained confidence at the school. I quickly became friends with many, although there were still a few at the school who I didn't like.

There was one school bully, who was vile. He once smacked me in my face laughing with his friends outside my uncle's house. I decided to hold my own, so I stood up and beat him in a fight that day. It wasn't long before I was out of control again at school. I never bullied anyone, and I never smoked or took drugs, but I did commit some crazy wrongful acts. I once trespassed onto the water companies' land opposite the school. I got into a tractor, found the keys, and began to drive it. There was also a bulldozer on the land that day, I found the keys in that too and drove it into the tractor smashing it up. I went back to school covered in mud. The police and the workers from the water company came to the school. It was obvious who had trespassed on the land, as I, and others were covered in mud up to the waistline. My father came to the police station to meet me. They took my picture and measured my height. My father was in tears at the police desk that day, but I was now of the age of criminal responsibility. This was the first serious matter of my life, but a lot more quickly followed, as not long after that I was arrested for shoplifting. I stole a Kinder Egg at a Woolworths store in Prescot. This turned out to be so much worse than shoplifting, as the police officer who took me home was my mum's friend from school. This caused her embarrassment. I was battered that day, and still remember my mum telling my dad that her hands hurt from hitting me. My dad replied, 'that's why I left the small end of a pool cue, hit him on the ankles with it.' The beatings became worse, and it wasn't long before I was in fear of returning home from school. My father would stand at the door and try to trick me by saying, 'We know what you have done today, so just tell us the truth and nothing will happen.' I would instantly look at his feet, to see if he had a slipper missing because that meant I was going to be hit with the missing slipper that would be hidden behind his back.

I ran away from home a few times, and once ran to my uncle's house in Prescot. My uncle on my dad's side was my dad's younger brother and he was married with two children. Sadly, he got divorced and his ex-wife and son moved far away, which made it difficult at times for my uncle to get to see his son. I loved this uncle very much; he was funny and would do anything for anyone. I remember watching him play football at Whiston, and he would call himself, 'the goal machine'. I stayed at my uncles for a week, due to how the beatings were getting worse. My dad had two brothers and a sister, his youngest brother had no children and never got married, he has worked at the same factory for forty years. My dad's sister had many children, but sadly, I have never met most of them. I must have gone twenty-five years without ever seeing my dad's sister, but I recently managed to get in touch with her young twin girls, just to offer any form of support that I can. My dad's side of the family were very different to that of my mum's family. I finally returned home from my uncles and tried my best not to misbehave. I attended the boxing club at Page Moss twice a week. This would use up my energy in a productive manner. I also attended Kensington Chess club, and I would get the bus on my own, even from a very young age. I first started playing chess at Parkview, as we had it as a lesson. The teacher was Mr. Curry, and I quickly grew fond of chess. I was extremely excited that a chess club started at Prescot High School. The teacher who started the chess club was my all-time favourite teacher and he probably doesn't know that. He cared about all pupils and had a real passion for math and chess. He made me chess captain; he even visited my home to recommend a chess computer to my parents that would assist my improvement. He attended the same chess club at Kensington, and he still attends the same club I represent today at Liverpool.

I continued to misbehave at school but looking back I do feel the teachers made matters worse, as in most classes I was not allowed to sit with others. I would often have a table and chair outside the classroom and the door would be left open for me to hear what was going on. Some teachers would do this before I even did anything wrong. Looking back, it was wrong as I believe I was victimised at times. The way I was made to feel would encourage me to bunk off from school, bunking off means to leave the school without making anyone aware. I would walk across the fields towards Knowsley Safari Park and simply roam about. Sometimes I would get the bus into Liverpool and beg for money. Once I received any money I would go straight to the arcade and play on the bandit machines. I was once handed a pound note by a middle-aged male. I told him I lost my bus fare home. I went to the arcade and won the jackpot. I won on a few machines that day and walked around Liverpool feeling like a millionaire. I bought a load of cakes from a bakery and sat outside St George's Hall eating them. I loved people watching, even from a young age and would sit outside St George's Hall when bunking off and watch the people passing by wondering where they were from and where they were going to. I started to behave at school, and I feel that this was down to the number of after school activities I had which were keeping me focused. I also started to box at a new club in Kirby. This was a club my dad's friends recommended. It was an amazing club, and it was a chance for a new start to boxing, as the club at Page Moss wasn't going well for me. My last two amateur fights before leaving ended in disaster, as I vomited with nerves. I know why this was, it was the amount of pressure put on me. My mother would apply so much pressure on me to do well, and even saying if you win, we will give you money, but if you lose, don't come home.

I would become so nervous; it was very off putting and ruined the experience. In the new club my parents very rarely came to see me, as it was much further away from the local boxing club and from where I lived. I enjoyed getting the bus to the new boxing club and I made new friends quickly when visiting Kirby. The bus journey would pass through Knowsley Village where I would often hang out with friends who lived there. School was going well too, as I started dating the most attractive girl in school. I had my first date; we went to the Cannon Cinema opposite Lime Street Station. I was wearing one of my dad's old suit jackets and a well-polished pair of school shoes.

I had a massive number of coins in my pockets which I earned from penny for the guy. As we entered the cinema, my girlfriend immediately stood beside the cashier window and expected me to pay for her too. I was fifteen pence short. It was embarrassing that I had to ask her for fifteen pence. Once the movie finished, we walked down to the Albert Dock, and on the way, we passed a McDonalds. I told her that I was sorry that I had no money to buy her a burger. We made our way to the waterfront, and we sat on a bench and looked out at the ship's passing by. She turned to me looking upset and said, 'I wish I could get on that ship and sail away and never come back'. She was dealing with upsetting matters at home that I was unaware of at the time. Looking back now it makes me upset to think what she must have been dealing with. Thankfully, I heard a year or so later, a lot came out and she was made safe from it all. All was going well, but sadly, this good behaviour would soon end, as I committed an act that would be my most dangerous act to date, and an act that ended any possible progress at the school. It was during October, and I was handed a large rocket at school.

This was a very dangerous firework, and one that had extreme power. We had a science mock assessment that day, and there were a lot of Bunsen burners being used. The science teacher walked past me, I lit the firework and threw it towards the teacher, giving no thought to the dangers or thinking about the consequences that would follow. The firework produced lots of smoke and made loud screaming noises. Everyone in the classroom was screaming with fear. The firework made its way from the floor towards head height and so everyone kept low, hiding under the desks.

The firework then made its way towards the large classroom window and smashed its way through it. The school called the police and fire brigade. The smoke quickly exited through the smashed window, yet the teacher told everyone to stay still and stay seated. I was surprised at this since there could have been hazards within the classroom. The firemen only visited for a few moments and left. The police asked everyone to stand and began to search the pupils. I emptied my pockets and there was a box of matches. I was taken into a small room and questioned by a police officer. It is only now being educated in law that I realise how badly the police handled the matter. I was instantly suspended from school whilst an investigation took place. I was invited back several weeks later when it was decided I would be expelled and would have to attend The Unit at Huyton Village. The Unit was a small set of huts that badly behaved children would attend for a set period. It resembled a prison sentence; I began to get upset at the thought I would not complete my GCSEs. I had been preparing for my GCSEs and was excited at the thought that they were less than a year away. Little did I know that I would never return to Prescot school again. The head handled it all very badly, and in hindsight I should not have been expelled as.

I feel that schools have a duty to care and teach children. If a child has extra needs, then the school should provide such, not just get rid, as that resolves nothing. I knew I had intelligence, as I won the schools chess championship against several schools. I was too embarrassed to stand up and receive my trophy by the director of chess in schools and so my schoolteacher got up and received it on my behalf.

The central oller was not created during the time of this picture.

Chapter Three

No more school

I will never forget the fear I had during my first visit to the Unit. I was told I would have to attend for twelve weeks. These would have been the last twelve remaining weeks of normal school. On my first day I was left traumatised, as I witnessed another boy pulling a girl's hair. She turned around with fire in her eyes and said in a very aggressive tone of voice, 'pull my fucking hair again and I will stab the fuck out of you.' The boy started to laugh, but not for long as she attacked him with a pencil, striking him on his shoulder with it. I sat in silence; I was crying inside. I had a feeling of failure running through me, I couldn't understand how I ended up in The Unit surrounded what appeared to be crazy out of control kids. There was a pool table and other activities for the kids to play. Including a table tennis table at the Unit. We would go outside to the field at the rear of the building, which today is an Asda car park. I remember my first outside activity day. We were to play rounders, at the start one of the boys picked up the bat and the teacher shouted across towards him saying, 'you are not allowed to hold the bat, as we know what happened last time with it.' I froze with fear and asked the girl beside me, 'what happened last time?' She replied, 'He hit someone on the head with the bat and the police came to take him away.'

At the end of my first week, I was at home crying to my mum, begging her not to send me back there. I was learning nothing, and any possible academic achievements were becoming impossible. I finally left the Unit and began to look for work. I bumped into a few pupils from my old school. They all seemed happy, as they were excited knowing that they were due to receive their GCSE results. I walked home that day in tears, as I thought I was worthless, and that I had become nothing. I was just a scruffy jobless young man with no hope and no qualifications, it was a horrible feeling. Things got worse due to the friends I started to hang out with from Page Moss. They smoked cannabis, but I refused to ever smoke it, thanks to boxing I was petrified of drugs. We ventured into Liverpool one Friday night and I was asked to hide cannabis in my coat due to me having a secret pocket in my hood. As we walked through the alleyway behind the Empire Theatre, a police car suddenly appeared, and police officers got out and began searching us. They found the cannabis and arrested me for possession, even though it wasn't mine. I was shouting at the officer whilst he drove. He became angry and got out of the car, coming at me in an aggressive manner. I got to the police station and was too scared to provide my parents' details, so I gave my grandparents details on my father's side. These grandparents were used to dealing with the police, and I had the idea that they may look out for me, but they informed my dad. My parents attended the police station, and I knew instantly that I would be in for a beating, even though the officer stated that there will be no need for them to take the matter further, as my parents would be handing out the punishment. He was laughing as he said this to me. I was more scared of my parents than the police. I didn't want to leave and at one point I asked the officers if I could stay.

Things started to change for me over the coming months, as there was an introduction to the Youth Training Scheme. I had the opportunity to work as an apprentice mechanic. This would be my first real job. I worked at the garage near Wilson Road, Huyton. It was freezing on my first day and I can still almost feel the wind as I look back. I wore my new steel cap boots and thick overalls. The owner's son appeared to have a drink problem, as he would drink pint after pint during lunch hour. The owner also had a drink problem and during my first week he approached me drunk and told me that during his first day as an apprentice he was taken into the corner by his boss and told he would get beaten up each Friday if the garage was not clean and tidy. I enjoyed working at the garage, as I was being allowed to do more and more as the weeks progressed. I was changing brake pads and discs. I was eager to learn as much as possible. The apprenticeship sadly came to an end due to funding. The garage could not afford me, and on my last evening the owner drove me home. He was drunk whilst driving and we mounted the pavement numerous times. My mum came outside, and he told her the sad news. My mum got upset, and I cried when I got indoors, as I was upset at the thought that I would not feel the cold or feel the oil and dirt on my hands which made me feel like a hard-working man. I couldn't stay at home and think about what plans I had next, as my father made me go to the fruit market with him each morning within a few days of my apprenticeship coming to an end. I would be given two shouts to get out of bed, and the third attempt would be a small bucket of water that would be thrown at me whilst I lay in bed. This was something I also experienced when I attended school, even at the young age of ten.

I would have to go to the fruit market before school, I hated it during the evening, as I had to turn my mattress upside down due to it still being wet from the morning soak. My parents were very strict with me, even at the age of sixteen. I would often receive physical punishment. The physical attacks continued and would only ever get worse, it still upsets me to this very day looking back. I finally got a job in the butcher's department at the Littlewoods store in Liverpool city centre. The building today is the Primark store. This was a great experience, as I enjoyed getting the morning bus. I had to arrive at work very early, as the butchers were one of the first to open. On my lunch break I would sit in the doorway and people watch. I was so proud to be wearing a works uniform, as it made me feel like a working and respected man. I worked at the butchers for six months before my final day loomed. I remember my last day; It was very upsetting. I was taken into a room and told I had to be let go, as someone was stealing and he was unsure who it was between me and another worker, so he was letting us both go. It wasn't me, and even today I look back in anger that I lost my role due to a thief that I was working with. It was extra upsetting as my young cousin ran towards me to meet me as I finished work that day. I held back the tears, so she and her sister didn't see me upset. Right now, at this stage of my young life I was feeling like a complete failure. It was as though I was being thrown from one place to another, experiencing nothing but disappointment and rejection. This made my parents more disappointed in me and I received more than the usual number of beatings during this time. I remember my sister crying and asking my parents to stop hitting me. My sister and I had fallen out a few times, but overall, I love her very much, and she is a very special person in my life. I have many fond memories looking back.

We once had a competition to see who could watch their favourite movie the most. I watched An American Werewolf in London over 120 times, and she was not far behind watching her favourite movie, The Wizard of Oz. There was one incident that reoccurs in my mind. I was lying on the sofa suffering badly with Glandular Fever. My sister appeared from the dining room with a golf club over her shoulder. She would have been around age six at the time. I said to her, 'Please, whatever you're thinking about doing, please don't do it.' She ignored my pleading and swung the club at me, catching me directly on the right knee cap. I jumped up in pain, and she instantly ran across the living room towards her Barbies and pretended to play with them. I deserved that attack, as a week or so before I locked her in a cupboard under the stairs and sang the Freddy song through the door. The Freddy song was from the horror movie, Nightmare on Elm Street. One of the funniest memories I have of my sister, was when I was around age 11, and my sister would have been approximately age 7. It was Christmas day, and my parents popped out to my grandmothers, leaving us alone for a short period. We jumped into one of my dads' cars and planned a trip to Wales. My father turned up as we reversed and asked us where we were going. I froze with fear, but my sister smiled and replied, 'We are off to Wales dad.' One of the most upsetting memories I have involved my sister. It was the day my mum had a huge argument with her sister at my grandmothers. As my mum was leaving, she shouted for me to leave too, but I wanted to stay. This made my mum angry, as it caused embarrassment in front of the family that she had just fought with. On our way home, my mum took all her anger out on me. She turned to me beating me and pulling my hair. I fell to the ground, and she kicked me.

My sister was screaming for her to stop. My mum would threaten me non-stop on our way home that day saying, 'the very moment we get in, you're getting battered lad.' I would walk in fear at the thought of the beating. I was upset mostly at the fact I had done no wrong. It was clear that she was taking her anger out on me, I was as good as a punch bag for her. As crazy as it sounds, I loved my mum very much, and she would stick up for me a lot. My mum would often show lots of affection and overall, she was a good mum most of the time, as she seemed to just want what was best for us. She would get angry when I did wrong, but this was because she wanted me to do well. It must have been hard for my parents as they were still very young, and I was bringing so much trouble to the door. I do regret so much from my childhood. The most valuable commodity we have is time, and I took time for granted. When we are young, we act as though we are going to live forever, as we pass up on so many opportunities. I took so much for granted looking back, and it still upsets me to this very day. I have so many regrets, I often look back and imagine completing my GCSEs at Prescot School. I picture myself smiling, surrounded by all my school friends, we are all waving our hands in the air with joy after receiving good results. I then sit with several pupils in the school grounds and discussed what college we wanted to attend but sadly, none of this happened, and instead, I would jump from job to job, getting nowhere fast. I didn't even get to complete high school, forced to leave several months early, and sent to The Unit. My parents' business was doing well and expanding at speed. This was mostly thanks to the hard work and dedication of both my parents. My parents finally sold their home at Gentwood and moved completely from Liverpool to a village in Warrington. Warrington is a town based in South Cheshire, even though Warrington is just forty-five minutes from Liverpool, I still had never visited the area.

The area seemed strange and uncomfortable to me, as we drove to our new home, I had a feeling that I didn't want to be there. I was missing Huyton. During my first week at the new home, I had enough and decided to walk to my grandmother's house. I was seventeen when moving to Warrington and I hated it. The walk to my grandmother's must have taken me hours. When I finally arrived, my grandmother was standing at the door laughing, asking me how long it took me. My parents had me working at the shop, but I still would argue with my mother and end up walking out, then end up making my usual journey to my grandmother's. My parents would not make it easy for me at home, as it was made clear I needed to work. I still attended the boxing club at Kirby and kept my fitness at full peak.

I would often travel back to Liverpool to visit my friends, but I eventually made friends at Warrington. There were a few nice lads in the road where I lived, two brothers in particular, I still see them today. I seemed to have excess energy built up inside me constantly, so I would often be found running in the nearby countryside. I was keen on fitness; my father always told me to stay fit. He came home drunk one evening back at Gentwood Road, saying, 'do not ever get fat lad.' One day coming home from work I spotted an advert for the Army. The pictures, showing young men with guns and soldiers running during physical exercise training all appealed to me. I popped into the army recruitment office at Warrington and joined up. I would have only been living at Warrington for less than a year at this point, and before I knew it, I joined the RCT division in the army, and basic training was to be held at Buller Barracks, Aldershot. The RCT stood for Royal Corps of Transport. I was excited at the thought and increased my training at the boxing club.

My fitness level was of a very high standard, and that was thanks to boxing from a young age. Exercise was second nature to me by now, as I had been running three miles without an issue from the age of eight, and then I would carry out multiple tasks at the boxing club once returning from runs. It was in the run up to joining the army and not surprisingly an incident occurred which almost prevented me joining. I was approached by a male in Warrington during night out. He grabbed me in a threatening manner, so I punched him in self-defence. The police visited my parents' home, but thankfully my parents were at work, and I managed to hide the whole incident. The police didn't charge me, as witnesses confirmed that I was the one who was grabbed. I thought I got away with it all, until my parents were having a meal in Warrington the following week, when a male served them a drink with a bandage on his face. My mum asked how he did it, and the male replied, 'It was your son.' My parents returned home, and I received a mouth full of verbal abuse.

I can only assume someone at the restaurant knew my parents and pointed them out to the male, as I have no idea how he knew who my parents were. I was upset at my parents for instantly assuming it was me who was to blame. It was the morning of leaving for the army. My parents took me to the train station, and I was extremely excited, but also upset about leaving my parents and sister. I had no real idea what to expect, but I had no fear about any of it at the same time. I was a confident young male, and at the peak of my fitness. When I was sitting on the train I thought about my family and all those evenings polishing my grandfather's shoes, and the skills I had developed which would now come in handy. The train journey to Aldershot was a lengthy one, I was told it would take around four hours.

This made me feel like I was moving to another country, it also made it more exciting, as it would be a location I had never visited. We were instructed to shave our hair so mine was shaved very short in preparation. My bag contained all what was on the list that the army provided, such as washing items, shoe polish, and much more. I had them all in my bag, plus a few extra items, such as my chess books and a small chess board to keep me occupied.

Chapter Four

From the army to the pool table

I finally arrived at Buller Barracks, and the excitement really started kicking in, as I could see that around ninety other recruits had arrived. We were all shown to our living quarters and informed that there would be a briefing shortly afterwards. There were six other recruits in my room, but it was a large room with large windows at one end and when entering the room, I made sure that I got the window side bed area. Not long after a Corporal walked in and started shouting for no reason whatsoever, and this instantly got my back up. I took a dislike to this Corporal immediately. The first words out of his mouth to me was, 'Scouser, get that shit off the floor and make your area tidy.' I replied with tone, 'My name isn't scouser.' I was then told to go outside and run around a small, circled area, which I thought was pointless. I ran around it with the positive thought that at least it was getting me away from tidying up. I was running around the area for approximately thirty minutes when the Corporal came outside to me shouting. He walked up to me and asked me If I had learnt anything. I replied, 'I have learnt that it takes around three minutes to run a complete lap.' He did not find my response amusing, as he marched me up to my room and ordered me to tidy my area, asking me to report to him once my task was complete. I made my area tidy, but I did not report to the Corporal as instructed, and instead I followed what the rest of the recruits had been told to do, which was to report to an area at the barracks to receive a kit. I received a uniform, which included boots, beret, combat clothes, and even an NBC suit. The NBC suit was for the possibility of being at war and dealing with Nuclear, Biological, and Chemical warfare. At times we had to run and exercise in these suits, and due to them holding in the heat, they would make the run extremely tough. The army wasn't for me from day one, as I simply couldn't handle the strict processes and procedures. I couldn't handle being shouted at, as I received enough of that at home. I had a chip on my shoulder, and it was as clear as day. Other recruits started to notice that I was a loose cannon, as they would say to me that I was crazy. I didn't look at myself as being crazy, I looked at myself as someone who just didn't like being spoken to badly. I wanted people to speak to me as I spoke to them, but the army didn't work like that. It was a place where you were spoken to badly and had to stay quiet and take it, and that was going to be a real issue for me.

The Corporal either forgot I was to report to him that day, or simply gave me a pass with it being the first day. The next few days was the settling in process. We were shown around the barracks, and everyone got to know each other. The Major at the barracks introduced himself and gave a speech that included a few words of advice on how to make it as a successful army recruit. His advice was to, 'stay anonymous.' Looking back this was very good advice, but sadly, I didn't take it, and in fact I did exactly the opposite, as almost all the non-commissioned officers knew who I was and knew my name for negative reasons. At the end of the first week, we were all taken into a large hall where it was explained to us that a table would be created to find out who was the fittest recruit, and on passing out that recruit would be handed a trophy. By week three I was on top of the leader board out of seventy-five plus recruits. I was comfortably clear. I was second out of all recruits in the two-kilometre race. The recruit who came first ran for his county. He was always going to beat me running, but he didn't come anywhere near me with upper body strength. Running with backpacks, again I won this without issue. The army even provided boxing gloves, and we would spar each week; I enjoyed this task for obvious reasons. My boxing ability shined, and this allowed me to move even more clear at the top of the table. By now I had made a positive name for myself in areas of fitness, but a negative name when it came to attitude. It wasn't long before I became involved in yet another incident. There was a recruit from London. He had a chip on his shoulder because during our second week I had beat him at boxing. He came at me in the hallway and threatened me, and without thinking I punched him. I didn't even say a word, I simply hit out. He fell to the ground and began to bleed. I was marched to a small building at the front of the barracks and told to wait. I was then placed into a vehicle and drove to a small building that had cells in it. I was placed in a cell for seventy-two hours before being released. I was told to take off my belt and beret, as I was not allowed to wear these items as they have the crown on them or something. I didn't really understand this, but I was soon marched to the Major's office. I was told to march into the room at speed whilst a Sergent Major was screaming in my ear. I was told I would receive a punishment that would last a few days. It was Corporal Johnson who would carry out the punishment, it was called a beasting. I had no idea what it was and went back to my room without a care in the world, but the next morning at 4 am I was woken up by Corporal Johnson who stated I was to join him for a run. Corporal Johnson had trained with the SAS, and we all knew how fit he was, he had amazing speed and strength when he had joined us on some of our runs. I was taken to a large hill, and he was shouting behind me to speed up. What Corporal Johnson and the army failed to realise with me was that I loved training, as it was all I knew. I loved getting woken up in the morning. I had experienced that all my life, at home it was tougher, as I got water thrown at me. That first morning it was cold, we had been running for ninety minutes before I noticed the Corporal was getting tired. I ran behind him, as he slowed down and shouted for him to speed up. He turned and hit me that morning and hit me real hard, and I flew back. I stood up and shouted, 'You wanna go?' He walked towards me and stated that he would hurt me badly and told me to stop instantly. He struck me again and I fell to the ground, but I got up and called him a 'shithouse.' There was no stopping a young kid with an attitude from Hillside at times. The third time he hit me, I couldn't breathe as he had hit my throat somehow. It was only then I decided to stay quiet as I was hurt.

When we returned, I overheard the Corporal talking to the Sergent. He said, 'He is one little fit bastard that one, it will take a lot to break him.' I started to feel that many had it in for me, and I became concerned that I would again be victimised, just like at school. The facts were, I deserved all what I was receiving. Two weeks from passing out which meant that you had completed basic training and now become a soldier, all the recruits were all allowed a day off, and lots were even allowed out of the barracks, but I wasn't. Instead, they picked me to play rugby, and I was to represent the NCOs. The NCOs are the Noncommission officers, these being the Corporals, and Sergeants. I had never played rugby in my life. It was a rough day, and the officers did not mess about. I was left with bruises and a swollen face, but I did cause a serious injury to an officer, and he was sent off with a badly cut leg. The evening after the rugby match, we were all allowed to go for a drink with strict instructions that we were only to have one pint. I drank with a friend, who was a recruit like me, and we ignored the instructions. We drank many pints that evening which was not a great move, as it was the night that there was a bomb exercise. This meant that many soldiers would come running into our barracks with guns and gas masks screaming and shouting for us to grab our bomb bags and make way to the bomb area. The bomb bag was a bag of equipment at the end of our beds that we would grab in case of a bomb threat. The equipment was a gas mask and protective clothing. The bomb area was an area near the barracks in a field where we would assemble. I was lying in bed drunk and didn't move and this would be the last straw for me. The following morning, I was again marched before the Major. The Major took me to the fitness table and pointed out how impressed he was with how far ahead I was in the lead. He stated I would make a good paratrooper or infantry soldier. The Major also stated that he may ask my cousin to have a word with me, as he was aware my cousin was also in the army, and he was doing well, certainly a lot better than I was.

It never happened and my cousin never got to see me, which upset me, as I wanted to see him. I was informed that I would be back squadded for attitude. This meant I would join recruits who were starting week one. I was told I would not be receiving the fitness trophy. The Major told me that he had never moved a recruit back to week one for attitude. It was usually a process used for recruits who had issues with fitness. Within four weeks I was back on top of the leader board and again the fittest recruit out of all the new recruits, but my attitude appeared to be getting worse. It was not long before it was decided that I would receive a dishonourable discharge (DD) from the army for attitude. The Major called my mum whilst I was present in his office.

I nervously stood in his office, worried what my mum may say to him. He stated that the army didn't want me. He added it was a great shame as I possessed great levels of fitness. My mum apparently stated that she didn't want me either. I remember getting the train home, arriving at Lime Street station in Liverpool and immediately walking to the Crown Hotel pub next to the station. It was clear I had just left the army, due to haircut and the army bag I carried. I had my army savings in my pocket, and I sat in the pub drinking beer wondering what would be next for me. I was dreading going home that day. I could hear my mum screaming at me and calling me a failure and an embarrassment. I walked in, saw my sister in her school uniform and as she walked past me, she laughed. I was told to sit down whilst they educated me on the rules of the house.

Chapter Five

Meeting the Celebrities

Upon my return home, I was forced to work as soon as possible. I had only lived in the area approximately nine months at this point and still didn't really know anyone. I started work for my dad and it appeared to go well. The following summer we went on holiday to the Isle of Man. This was a favourite destination for the family and had been for many years. My grandparents went that often over the years that they appeared on a postcard at one point. My mothers' sisters and all my cousins would go. It was a great holiday, and It was lovely that the family were all together. During the last few days of the holiday, I was out walking alone and got talking to a girl who was on holiday with her family. We went for a long walk up to Bradda Head that day and we spoke what it would be like to work on the Isle of Man. She was due to start university but agreed to see if we could both work on the Isle of Man for the summer before she was due to start her studies. During the last few days of the holiday, I approached the hotel manager and asked if they had any jobs going. The hotel manager agreed to give me a role and during the last day of the family holiday I would say my goodbyes and stay. I ran to straight to the girl I met and made her aware that I had managed to get a job. She was happy and told me that she would return after the holiday and join me in working there for the summer. It was a nervous experience meeting the rest of the staff at the hotel. Most of the staff appeared to come from Northern Ireland. I instantly became friends with Tommo.

He was from Belfast, and I would enjoy listening to how life was like for him back home. My grandmother told me that my granddad worked selling ice cream on the Isle of man at one point and I would often try and picture my granddad selling ice cream as I walked along the seafront. I felt free on the Isle of man, but again it wasn't long before I started to get myself into trouble. I worked with Tommo behind the bar, and we would often sneak shots of whiskey and other spirits, which would result in us being drunk whilst working. The tips were good, and I would often go to the casino or play pool for money. I was very talented at pool and would often stay undefeated for over twenty games in a pub whilst playing winner stay on. This means the winner continues to play until they are beat. I was on the phone daily to the girl I met and excited at the thought of her joining me. The hotel I worked at became more and more crazy. Staff were allowed to run free; they were taking wine and spirits out of the hotel. The owner was drunk a lot and didn't seem to care. On a few occasions in one hotel I worked at, all the staff came out with large sums of cash. They shared it amongst other staff, and I was handed a bundle of notes. I didn't ask any questions and just walked away. I walked straight to the pub to play pool for money. The girl I met arrived, and she quickly became my girlfriend. We needed to look to see where we could live. We managed to rent a flat at Port St Mary, it was a great spot overlooking the harbour. My new partner in crime got a job in the local supermarket, and I would often walk down to meet her after work. I continued to work at the hotel, but it became more and more crazy there. One day after work I went to the local pub and played pool, I was winning a lot that night. I must have been around £150 up when a local lad shouted towards me aggressively, 'You're a scouse cheating bastard'. I turned and just headbutted him without a second's thought. My head started bleeding, so I hit out and punched him in the face. He flew to the floor and looked badly hurt. I then left the pub, but a large group started to chase after me. I ran back to the flat and climbed up to the window, as I had lost my key. My girlfriend looked out the window and became upset as I was covered in blood. I attended a clinic the following day and they dressed the wound and covered it up. When I went back to the pub the following day I was barred. This would be the end of me playing pool for money. I look back at that incident today and can't imagine what I was thinking. I was just young, drunk, and foolish. I am ashamed today looking back at most of my behaviour. There was nothing good or funny about it, nothing but shameful behaviour. I continued to work at the hotel for a few days before deciding to look for work elsewhere. I came across a job advertised at The Mount Murray Country Club. It was a sixty-minute walk from Port St Mary, but it was a lovely place. My girlfriend was still happy working in the supermarket, as she made friends there and was settled. I went for an interview at The Mount Murray, the same day I attended a second interview at The Castletown Golf Club. I didn't get the role at the Castletown Golf Club, but I was offered a role at The Mount Murray, and I accepted it. I would be working as a barman, as well as arranging tables for events, such as weddings etc. I kept in touch with Tommo and a few other Irish friends who I worked with at Port Erin, but a few of the Irish lads thought I was crazy I guess, and I would see them less and less. I had behaviour issues at that age looking back. I had no fear whatsoever of anything. It was best for me to avoid Port Erin for a while due to the trouble I got involved in. This was hard at times, as my girlfriend still worked at Port Erin, and I would often meet her after work, walking with her back to the flat. I also enjoyed the sandwiches at the Port Erin train station and would often pop there, but as I became more comfortable working at The Mount Murray,

I would visit Port Erin less and less. The one great thing with the Isle of Man is the TT races. I met with Tommo a few times and we decided to walk to Douglas from Port Erin whilst the TT races were racing. The bikes would pass by at crazy speeds. We had to walk through the fields to get to Douglas, as all the roads were closed due to the races. We walked on the road at times, and men in high vis jackets would scream for us to get off the road. A split second later a bike would pass by at high speed, you could instantly smell burning rubber. It was scary being so close as a bike passed at high speed. Since 1995 The Isle of Man has built a worldwide reputation, having co-financed and co-produced over one hundred feature films which have been filmed there. Whilst I worked on the Isle of Man a few movies were being made, and TV programmes. My first few days at The Mount Murray were enjoyable. The Hotel was of a much higher standard too that of the hotel I worked previously. It was much cleaner, and the décor was lovely. The customers who visited the golf course were all respectful people. The weddings held at the club never had issues or trouble either. Overall, it was a nice working environment. There were many actors and production team members staying at the hotel side of the club. I would often serve coffee during the mornings and alcohol in the evening. I started to really enjoy my time at The Mount Murray, and I settled in well. I was placed at the bar located at the 18th hole. This bar area served sandwiches, and I would often have free sandwiches for my lunch, as there was no charge to staff. I would often call my mum and grandmother telling them about the people who I met. My grandmother loved the Isle of Man, so she was always interested to hear how I was getting on. I would have to work until the last resident left the bar area. I would work until 3 a.m. some evenings.

The last bus was around 11 p.m., so I missed the bus most of the time and would have to walk home or hitchhike. The walk would take me around ninety minutes. It was a nice walk home, as no one was about. I would walk along the seafront listening to the waves crashing against the rocks. I would always be daydreaming as I walked, picturing what my life would be like in years to come. I always pictured myself married with children. I remember I once sat at the bus stop waiting for the bus unaware that I had already missed it. I sat there daydreaming away and even wrote a message on a scrap of paper for my future children. I wrote, 'I love you very much, and I am a proud father. This was the bus stop where your father waited after work.' I wrapped it up in a bit of plastic and buried it next to the bus stop. I was always daydreaming about what the future had installed for me. There were a few incidents during my working time at The Mount Murray. I would often have a few drinks behind the bar, which was obviously a no, no. I also argued with the manager of the bar on one occasion. He was from Northern Ireland, and around thirty-five years old. He took his job way too seriously. He seemed to enjoy ordering staff about, so I would avoid him as much as possible. This wasn't difficult as he very rarely came to the bar area I worked at, but on one occasion he ordered me to attend the bar located on floor one. I entered the room and there would be and another young male working behind the bar. We were informed that filming would be taking place during the time we were working, so we had to stay very quiet. They were filming a show called Antiques Hunt, or something very similar to that. The person hosting the show was lovely, there was also a male who I recognised from a few TV programmes. They had placed silver looking tin foil on the ceiling, I assume to create lighting maybe. There were lots of cameras and all was silent up to when they stopped for a break. It was a break for us too, as we could then make a little noise and move about. The female host came to the bar and asked for red wine and a Bloody Mary for the male expert. I had no Worcester Sauce that day, but I noticed some soy sauce left over from an event the previous evening. I poured on soy source, thinking he wouldn't notice. The director shouted, 'action.' The male expert spat out his drink and came to the bar upset asking me what I had put in his drink. I told him it was Worcester Sauce. He replied, 'I have been drinking this drink for many, many years, and that was not Worcester Sauce.' I replied, 'Ah, you see we are in the Isle of Man and Worcester Sauce is different here, as it doesn't travel very well, ya see.' This didn't go down well, as five minutes later I was ordered to leave the bar area and work at a different bar. I was told many years later that my grandfather often told people this story at pubs he visited, as he found the story very amusing. I often tell the story myself, and I even tweeted the host from the show, telling her the story. She replied to me, stating that it was funny. I would enjoy watching the actors enter the bar area after their breakfast.

They would enter the bar area for a coffee and sit to read their scripts or morning newspapers. I became fascinated with one actor; he was one of the main characters in a movie that was being filmed. He was a lovely gentleman and clearly an amazing husband, as he was lovely towards his wife when they were together. I would watch him and could see that he was a lovely man, as stated, not all were lovely, but this guy was top of the list. One evening I was working until 5 a.m. as several actors didn't leave the bar area. The actors didn't pay for their drinks, it was all free and paid for by the production company. They simply stated their room number, and it was billed to their room. I finished work and was very tired. I fell asleep for a few hours in the bar area when I woke up thinking I'd

best get home as my girlfriend may be worried about where I was.
I was approached by the hotel manager asking me if I would be
interested in a couple of hours' work. I only had to hand out scripts
to the actors' rooms. I agreed and the first room I went to, was the
elderly gentleman who I was a fan of. He came to the door wearing
a white dressing gown. He smiled and handed me a twenty-pound
note, I thanked him and ran as fast as I could to the next room
hoping for more tips. I can still picture that morning, and the smile
he gave me; he was a great guy. I became friends with a few local
lads who were working at The Mount Murray. This was a good
move for me, as they introduced me to a few hidden away gems.
During our day off we all walked to a local woodland. The locals
took us to a diving spot, that I can only describe as a massive well.
We climbed up the side of the rocks and jumped into the rounded
well-like pool. It was impossible to touch the bottom, the depth
must have been extreme. The water was ice cold, and it was a long
walk home that day, but my clothes soon dried as I walked. This
was the advantage with working during the summer season. The
weather was lovely most of the time.

I continued to work at The Mount Murray and my girlfriend
continued to work at the co-op. We only ever seemed to work and
had very little time off. I did have a habit of getting on a bus without
a clue where I was going. I would get off and have a drink in
whatever pub I came to first. I would often end up talking to total
strangers, telling them about my parents. I was very proud of my
dad and would often tell people about him and what he had
achieved. One afternoon, I got talking to a psychic at one pub. She
was a very old woman and stated that I would fall in love very fast,
get married and have three children. I asked her would I ever come
back to The Isle of man, she replied, 'Yes, you will come back, but

you will never visit again until you next pop back with your wife.'
I said, 'what about my kids?' She then said something that sent a
shiver through me. She went on to say, 'You will not come with
your first wife, but with your second wife.' I sat there feeling sad,
she told me not to worry and went on to say that I was too good for
my first wife. She told me that I was a good lad, but I made a lot of
mistakes. She finally told me that I would suffer one day, and it
would live with me for many years, and change who I am, but not
to worry, as I would finally get over it all and get back to being me
again. I always wondered what she meant by this, I assumed she
meant that it would be the death of a family member maybe, but
now I think it could be true, as it was so very accurate. I suffered
PTSD for over ten years after being shot, and it changed who I was.
I was married and had three children, and what is even more scary
is the fact that I have never been back since. I was offered a job
role to revisit the following summer, and it was all booked and
planned, but I didn't end up going. Little did I know that just two
years from that moment I would be shot and dying on a pub floor.
I have never been back to the Isle of Man, which is my favourite
place, and it seems strange really when I think about it. I was dating
a girl after my divorce and we booked a trip to the Isle of Man, but
I got a flat tyre on the way home from work and we missed the trip.
It is all strange that I have not been back, and I often sit and wonder
when I will next visit. Tommo decided to share the flat with us, but
he didn't last long. He was soon back staying at the hotel. The area
staff lived in wasn't the best and I was shocked he went back. Me
and my girlfriend continued to stay at the flat and would often have
a few days out together. We once decided to go into Douglas and
visit the casino. I had a few hundred pounds to spend, as I made a
lot of money when working and receiving tips. I was also handed
money from a member of staff who had some scheme going and

asked me to not say anything. I think he used to only state one sandwich was sold instead of two. I should not have accepted the money at all, as getting arrested would not have been worth it. We went to Douglas and entered the casino. I started to win on the reel roulette and won nearly £900. My girlfriend was getting worried I may start to lose and asked me not to bet anymore and leave, she was correct too. She was a great girl; she was very sensible and had amazing parents. She was brought up well. Her mum was once a headmistress at a Liverpool school, if I remember correctly. She certainly had that appearance, as I felt scared in her company, as though I was near authority, I do remember her mum being an amazing cook, as the food I had whilst visiting my girlfriends' parents was probably the best food I have ever had. I continued to bet that night in the casino, and I began to lose. I lost all my winnings, and we left feeling sad. We started to walk that night but ended up getting a taxi. When you came out of the casino you could see where there was once a large building. I was told by my uncles and grandmother that there had been a terrible incident that took place there. My uncle told me that many people died in a disaster at Douglas, and I remember as he told he looked sad. My family may have even been at the Isle of Man during the time it had happened. When I researched it, it really was a very upsetting incident, as fifty people had lost their lives in a fire. The summer was ending, and my girlfriend was getting ready to leave, she was getting ready to attend university at Stoke. She went home and I was very sad to see her go. I stayed on a while before I also decided to go back home. Her parents once visited my parents' home, and I would stay at her home on occasions. She was from Rochdale, but now lives in Norfolk. When I arrived home from the Isle of Man, I didn't like where my parents lived. I never settled in Warrington at all, so I decided to go and live with my girlfriend whilst she was at university. I arrived and she was in a shared house with three other students, who were far from nice. My girlfriend made it clear she wanted to move out of the house and get a house with me instead. The students didn't want her to leave and refused to allow her to have her belongings. I got angry at this and visited the house and demanded her property to be returned. There were a few males at the door that day, but I still kicked the door open and got her belongings. There was hardly any damage to the door that day and I walked away peacefully, but several weeks later I was arrested for criminal damage. I didn't care at all, as I knew it was them who were the nasty people. I was not allowing them to cause upset. We moved into a couple of houses before settling in a house with lovely students who shared it with us. I started to look for work straightaway so I could contribute towards the bills and so I contacted a few work agencies and managed to get work at Michelin tyres. It was a horrible job stacking tyres. The smell of the rubber would make you feel sick. I finally got work at Yates Wine Lodge and felt much more at home working in a bar. This was what I was used to, and I quickly became friends with all the staff. I started to play snooker opposite the post office in Hanley. I had to walk up lots of stairs to get to the snooker centre. This is where I first met Dave Deakes. He was a great man, and very well liked. He would often take me to one side and tell me how bad betting was. I took his advice as much as possible, as he was right about betting. I once cashed six £50 cheques at the bar and bet all the money and lost. The cheques bounced and I was too ashamed to show my face at the bar again. I finally went to the bar and Dave took me to one side. He was upset, and I was upset that I let him down. I paid him the money back and was allowed to continue playing at the snooker centre. I explained I didn't do it on purpose, and I really did think that the cheques would clear, as they had a

£50 guarantee on each cheque, and I dated the cheques on different days. The snooker centre was an amazing place. I would often walk home late in the evening. I remember cutting across Hanley Park, but this turned out to be a dangerous move, as local Asian gangs would wait for white students and attack them. I was once chased by a group from a gang, but thankfully I made it away. I would pop home back to Warrington from time to time and became addicted to hitchhiking. It was so easy. I simply stood near the motorway, and I would get a lift home without fail. I did the same in the Isle of Man at times and it never failed. I would get to talk to interesting people, and they would ask me why I was hitching a ride and where I had been. Looking back, it was foolish and dangerous. I would never advise anyone hitching a ride due to the amount of scary people there are these days. The Isle of Man was fine back then, as they were all local people who were nice and there was very little crime committed on the island. Me and my girlfriend started to go our separate ways. We kind of ended the relationship without officially stating it was over. I could not and would never say a bad word about her. She was and I am sure that she still is an amazing person, who as stated, was from an amazing family. I often look back with a smile at the memories we had with each other. She did visit me at Burtonwood on one occasion and it was lovely seeing her again. I have not seen her since and hope her life is going well. It was now time for me to return home to my parents. This would always be the part I dreaded, as my parents made life so hard living at home. My parents had a third child, and it was as though they were having a new start. The start didn't seem to involve me or my sister. We appeared to be treated less favourably than the youngest sibling. I loved my brother even though he was clearly favoured. I remember that every pay cheque I received when working I would buy him as much as I could afford such as track suits, football boots, trainers, all kinds. My mum once laughed at my dad saying, 'Leave him to buy it, as we save money.' Looking back, I know now that this attitude was disgusting behaviour. If your son is working hard, not getting into trouble you should reward them with a happy environment and not take advantage of them. My father once shouted at me aggressively saying, 'He is my son, not yours.' This was my dad's reaction when I walked into the house with tracksuits for my brother. My parents were a strange pair, and very aggressive a lot of the time. My sister was at secondary school when I returned from Stoke and had her own life with her friends. I have always thought of my sister as though she is still that little girl at Parkview school running around with huge curly brown hair, but as she grew, we would spend less and less time with each other.

Chapter Six

Warrington Life

I have never been a fan of Warrington, as it has never felt like home. I just preferred going back to Liverpool, as it has always felt like my real home. I got a job at JJB sports in Warrington upon my return home from Stoke. It was there I discovered that I possessed an ability to sell. People would come into the store and ask for me personally. I would sell extras when people purchased trainers, such as shoe cleaner. I even set a record for the most shoe cleaners sold and due to this I was asked by the area manager to give a demonstration to other stores about how I put forward my shoe cleaner selling pitch. I started to feel I was under achieving at JJB, so I started to look for a more suitable job role. I applied for a sales role at Rumbelows. It was a large store that sold electrical appliances including TVs and stereos. I again set a record, this time, for the most extended guarantees sold by a single salesman. I was approached and asked how I was selling so many extended guarantees. The store manager and area manager even had concerns that I may have been adding the extras without the customers' permission, but this was certainly not the case. I guess it was just hard for them to believe that someone so young was so good at selling. I hit the floor running in my new role and became friends with some of the staff at the store. My life appeared to be turning around, and I was heading in the right direction for once.

The abuse inflicted by my parents sadly continued. I returned home from work one afternoon and my parents told me to sit down as they needed to talk with me. They said I needed help and that they had contacted a medical professional. They contacted a mental department at Winick, I believe. They had arranged an appointment for me to be assessed. The meeting was held at a building next to Warrington hospital and not at Winwick where I dreaded going. I was at the meeting for five hours. They completed tests for ADHD, Autism, and many other mental illnesses. The assessment finally came to an end, and I was told that I suffered no mental illness. They added that I was actually a very intelligent young man. They went on to state that their concern was with my parents and for me to consider reporting any abuse I suffered. They also stated that they were considering referring such concerns.

I returned home and my parents began shouting saying, 'We bring them a full-on mental person and they allow him back into public. We wonder why the world is not a safe place anymore.' They would start laughing and think it was all amusing. It was far from a laughing matter, and I couldn't wait to get out of my parent's home and move away. I continued to job hop, and I finally left Rumbelowes. I struggled to settle in one role, but I would always find work at speed. I started working at an appliance warehouse and this ended up like my previous role at Rumbelowes. I didn't like the staff there, as they wanted to try act tough for some reason, and they were far from it. The manager was very annoying too. They had an issue with people from Liverpool for some reason. In this role we would keep cash in our pockets when customers paid for items. There was no till as such, and halfway through the day we would cash in with the manager. I went for lunch one day and dropped £30, I searched everywhere for it.

The only thing I could think of was to pop to the betting office and try to win the £30 back. I had over £1,000 takings from the store that day in my pocket. I gambled most of it and lost all the takings. They made me pay back the money each month out of my wages. Once the debt was paid, they fired me, but I was glad to see the back of the place and the idiots that worked there. I found myself getting more and more in trouble. I started to date a girl from the other side of Warrington. She was a terrible person, and her uncles were disgusting people who would threaten me. They would only do this when with their friends. It was a very strange family to say the least, and there was no shock that this girl had issues all her life with boyfriends. I started to go out drinking with a couple of the local lads from around Penketh. They were only ever interested in going out to town and drinking. I started to talk to a girl during a night out and my two friends were talking to her friends. We went back to the girl's house, and I was taken to her bedroom. I got in her bed, but a while later, I heard a voice, 'get the fuck out right now.' I turned around and a male hit me with a glass bottle. I hit out and punched one of the males in the face and began running down the stairs. There were more males standing near the front door. I again hit out, punching one of them. I opened the door fully and ran down the street. I was completely naked. I suddenly came to a dead end, so I jumped over the fence and ended up in a huge bunch of brambles, It was Great Sankey canal. I had to swim across the canal and get to the main road. Once I was on the main road I started jogging down the side, on the grass verge, cars were beeping as they passed. I finally got home and had to climb through my bedroom window. My father opened my bedroom door and witnessed me halfway through the window completely naked.

He shouted my mum, 'Love, you won't fucking believe this, I knew he was on drugs, he is fucking naked here hanging out the window.' I went straight to sleep and woke up in much pain due to the cuts caused from the brambles. My friends attended my parents' home and were all laughing. I knew I needed to sort my life out, but I had no plan. I was still young and still very much obsessed with the nightlife and town centres. During a night out at Mr Smith's nightclub, Warrington, I met a girl from Liverpool, and we got on well with each other and started dating. It wasn't the best of relationships, as we split up every four weeks. Her mother became tired of it all and fed-up with my girlfriend bringing all her belongings back and forth. We started renting a flat at Great Sankey. It was going okay, but she was just very jealous, and I would always be accused of cheating. I did cheat on her, but just the once, and I was caught red handed. I was driving my girlfriend's car, with my ex-girlfriend, who was sitting in the passenger seat, when suddenly, my current girlfriend crossed the traffic lights and noticed us. She ran at the car kicking it and she never trusted me after that and rightly so. She tried to get me back one Friday when calling me as I was out with my friends at Liverpool. She said, 'I am cheating with a guy at the hotel near work right now.' This was a terrible thing to say, we were both young and saying and doing silly things. It was all immature behaviour that was of no help to anyone. I drove to the hotel and asked the receptionist if anyone by that name was staying and she replied, 'yes' and provided me the room number. I ran to the room, and noticed next to the room was a ledge. I thought it was a better idea to climb on the roof and look through the window, so I could catch them red-handed.

I climbed on the very high roof, hurting myself, as there were spikes attached to the building that I caught my legs. I got to the window and forced it open and began to climb through. It was the wrong room, a male and female jumped out of bed and started screaming for help. I quickly jumped back out, apologising on my way out. I ran as fast as I could, but police were quickly on the scene as I spotted them in the distance making their way to the hotel. The next day I my girlfriend called who said, 'that was you last night wasn't it? You mad bastard.' This all sounds like funny little adventures, but I would often sit at home and get upset, as I knew this behaviour was getting me nowhere fast. I ended the relationship with this girlfriend as her mum called the police. Her mum lied to the police saying I followed her to work when I didn't, and I was handed a caution at the court in Bootle, Liverpool.

This girl would often still try get in touch with me from time to time, she even visited me at hospital when I was shot, but didn't approach me that day, she just looked in from the ward entrance. I never wanted to get back with this girl, as her mum was trouble and I asked her to leave me alone as I already had to attend court for something I didn't even do, so she finally moved out the flat and went home. I couldn't afford the rent on my own when we split up, so I went home to my parents, but they didn't want me staying there. I still remember the night I went to my parents' home. I knocked on the door with my push bike and a black bin bag full of clothes. My mum and dad answered, saying to me, 'We are going to do something that one day you will thank us for. We are going to turn you away; you are not wanted here please go away and start a new life somewhere far away.'

There was a police car at the bottom of the pathway, as there were some youths on the field near my parents' land. A police officer overheard my mum shouting and approached the pathway, my mum instantly asked the officer to make me leave and go away. I will never understand how any mother could turn her son away like that. I had never taken drugs or hurt anyone, nor was I a danger to anyone. I began to walk, and the black bin bag began to rip open, spilling my clothes over the floor. I walked to the nearby field and tried to make a bed with my clothes on top of my bike. I slept that evening in the field, and It was scary, as I could hear rats moving through the tall grass. I lasted homeless for nearly two weeks, before I was offered a room above a chip shop. I was also offered a job as a manager of a local Spar supermarket; this was good money. I was handed a lot of responsibility, and it wasn't long before I was living comfortably, but I soon started to get into trouble at the local pub. I was, for some unknown reason, getting drugs from my friend, and because I didn't take drugs, I handed them to another person in the pub who gave me money. I was basically dealing drugs without even knowing it. This was the start of something extremely dangerous. I started to go to Liverpool more and more. I started dating a girl from Knotty Ash, she was an amazing girl, from a lovely family, and she also had a good job as an air hostess. She is my one regret I have, as it was a chance of having a real decent relationship with someone and building a life with her, but I messed it all up by being an absolute loser. I was introduced to a few people in Liverpool. One male who knew people who I was friends with took a liking to me, he seemed impressed with who were my friends at the time. He asked me about drugs and asked me if I could get five thousand pills. I told him yes; I knew a lad who is involved in that stuff; I didn't think any wrong is getting people to talk between each other.

I was told that the pills would cost £1.50 each and would sell for £2.50. This would be a £5,000 profit for the lad I knew, and simply work for him, in simply passing on a bag, but things are never that simple. The evening came that the deal would take place. I received a call asking if I could provide a lift. I only said yes, as the guy who was selling the drugs stated he had free nightclub event tickets for me that he didn't need no more. I ended up going along, and ended up in a house in Kensington, Liverpool. There were seven huge lads standing in the room. They were asking me if I wanted to buy any guns. They also told me that they thought I was sound and invited me out to a few nights out around Liverpool. They handed the lad who was with me the bag of pills. The lad I knew approached me, handing me the tickets, and laughed saying, 'you taking this risk giving him a lift just for tickets, you're a mad bastard,' and I was, I mean, why was I even there at all? I decided to walk out at that point; We drove to Warrington, and a police car appeared behind us, my heart sank. I was shaking like a leaf but managed to keep driving in a calm manner. I drove to the drop off point, and the other male handed the bag over and received the bundle of cash. The lad I was with gave me a few hundred pound as a thank you for giving him a lift. A lift that I thought was a good thing, a good thing to be around, a bit of excitement and an adrenaline rush, but a lift that could have destroyed my life for nothing. I remember sitting at Liverpool docks asking myself, 'what the hell was I thinking.' I started to cry in anger, as I was feeling like the world's biggest idiot. I could have gone to prison for many years. My life would have been over and for nothing. I told the lads I didn't want any more part in being around anyone who deals drugs. They agreed and understood, but one male asked me for one last favour. He asked me for a lift from Huyton to Liverpool. I agreed thinking nothing of it, he put a huge bag in my boot and told me to meet him at his house in Liverpool. He handed me £100 fuel, so I started to drive. I stopped halfway and inspected the bag. It was the size of a large suitcase, and full of pills. This could get me over 10 years in prison if caught. I dropped the suitcase off and drove away as fast as I could. I remember that evening because I drove to Wales and sat at the seafront going over my life and wondering how I had got myself in this position. The following week I told a few of my mates from Bootle. They were angry that this other lad took advantage of me. They approached him and threatened him. They shouted, 'He isn't involved in your shit, don't ever ask him for a lift for your shit again and stay away or you are going to get fucked up.' He never contacted me again after that, as they knew my mates were not people you'd want to mess with. I swore to myself that I would never get involved in drugs again or go near people who was involved in such either. I look back disgusted in myself, as It would have only taken for a police car to pull me over and check the car. I would have lost my life at that very moment and for nothing. It is simply not worth it, and if anyone states that it is worth it, they are fools and nothing else. Drugs kill thousands of people each year. Thankfully today and since a young age, I am very anti-drugs. I needed to get my life on track and fast. I knew it was best to continue working, and I had a good job role, which would assist me in building a good credit rating. I finally applied for a mortgage, so that I would have a secure home. I was accepted for a mortgage thanks to the good job I had as a store manager. I purchased a terraced house at Burtonwood, Warrington. I lived alone and it all seemed to be going well, except that I attracted bad people to me once again. Lads would always want to be my friend, and I always made friends at speed. My current girlfriend was amazing, and it was crazy I didn't realise that at the time. I borrowed her car one evening, as I left clothes at an ex-girlfriend's house in the Wirral. I drove, but whilst driving I was panicking for some reason. It was raining that evening, and a car pulled up beside me at speed as good as forcing me off the road. The car skidded down the side of a large embankment. It rolled over multiple times before hitting a horse. I thought for a moment that I killed the horse, but it got up after five minutes. It must have just been winded or knocked out maybe. I got out the car and climbed back up the embankment onto the main road. There were people standing in shock asking me if I was ok, and for some reason I started jogging away from them. I ran to a fence at the rear of a house and climbed over. I knocked on the door, with the idea of asking permission to call a taxi. An old lady answered and invited me in, she had another old friend sitting with her. The next minute, I am sitting having cake and tea with two pensioners talking about life. I called a taxi and got it to the nearest address I knew, and that was a previous girlfriend. Her brother agreed to give me a lift back to Warrington. I immediately called my girlfriend and told her what had happened. She was upset and rightly so, but she still came to see me, and we stayed at a hotel that night. I hate myself for ever upsetting her, as she didn't deserve any of that. Many months later, the police visited my house surrounding it and accusing me of causing a crash, even though there was no other car involved. I attended a solicitor to seek advice, and he attended the police station at Liverpool with me. No officer came and the solicitor stated for me to put my name down and leave. I left and twenty-seven years on I have still not heard nothing, and rightly so, as I did nothing wrong. I crashed, yes, but no one else was involved, only me. I soon split up with my girlfriend and it was upsetting for me. I wasn't good enough for her, as I was a loser and an idiot. I went home and sat there for hours hating myself. I would go on long walks feeling bad about myself and wondering where my life was heading. It was no shock that I soon lost my job role as a store manager. I didn't seem to care much, as I hated being at Warrington, and soon began looking for work again, but this time in Liverpool. I started to go out in Liverpool more and more, and eventually got a job at Liverpool city centre at a sports store. I drove a car that had no car tax on it, so I would always try to park the car outside Liverpool city centre, but during my first few weeks I couldn't find a parking space, so I drove into the city centre, and as I turned around in the road, I headed towards a barrier, when suddenly a security guard approached me asking, 'you work here lad, am sorry I will let you in to park, gis a sec lad.' He didn't give me the chance to tell him I was only turning around. I drove through and parked my car. I jumped over the wall, so the security guard didn't see me and ran into town to work. I did this for five months before someone asked me where I parked my car. When I told my friend, he began laughing hysterically, and he went onto to say, 'You park there as you no car tax? You any idea what that building is? It is the head office for tax, lad.' I started laughing and thought, only I could end up parking there. The job didn't last long as the pay didn't cover all I needed it to. I applied elsewhere, getting a job working in Yates Wine Lodge in the centre of Liverpool. This covered all the bills, as I was offered as much over time as I wanted, and I received tips. I made lots of new friends and it wasn't long before I started dating again. I started to date a young student, but it was casual dating, and we knew it wasn't going anywhere. I started to attend nightclubs on a regular basis. I would drive home afterwards, which was foolish to say the least. I was on board a ride that could be named, 'a loser's life.' I just sat there and went along with it all. Some friends started visiting me at my home. I knew they were not the best of lads, but again I just went along with it all. I started to attend pubs all over Liverpool, and at Speke, which is located at south Liverpool. I went here with other friends I knew from Runcorn. This was a rough area; my mates were all doormen at the pubs there. I overheard that there was a war going on between doormen and landlords. There had been many shootings related to it all and for some reason it didn't scare me as much as it should have done. I started to have car trouble, so I started hitchhiking to Speke. I used to carry a petrol can, and people would stop, thinking I had broken down. I would get to the pub quicker than my friends would drive there. It all seemed okay the way I was living, and I didn't think anything of it. I didn't see any wrong with the people I was associated with and looked at everyone as good friends. I would go out drinking late and end up at different girls' houses drunk. I would always struggle getting back home to Burtonwood, as it was in the middle of countryside and forty minutes from Liverpool city centre. I became friends with a woman from Winchester who I met during her visit to Liverpool. She was married to a Nuclear Submarine commander. They had a massive house, which had tennis courts and surrounding grounds. She wanted to sleep with me, but it didn't happen, as I didn't look at her in that way, she was just more of a friend. We would sit and go over the mistakes I had made in life, and she would ask me if I was dealing drugs. I told her the truth. I made it clear I had passed on drugs in a pub on occasions and each time the value was around £20. I only passed it onto someone else not thinking anything of it. I also told her that there was a couple of occasions when I drove someone who collected drugs and only went along as I was promised free nightclub tickets, and another occasion I had drugs in my boot, but that time, I didn't know what was in the boot of the car. We spoke about how bad and wrong drugs are and we both agreed that I had been very foolish and naïve. I simply didn't think or take into consideration any possible consequences.

I sat and near cried with frustration on the train ride home from Winchester. I hated who I was and how foolish I had been. I would always think of my grandma and how ashamed she would be if she knew the truth. Saying that, I could kill four hundred people, and my grandma would still say I was innocent, as I could do no wrong in her eyes. I needed to change, but I had no plan of action with how to change and how to escape the circle I was part of. The circle that involved nightclubs and late-night parties. I had no one else in my life and would only become bored when spending periods of time on my own. I messed up the chance of a decent relationship, I had messed up so much up to this point of my life. It was hard for me to escape the life I was living, as I knew no one else and only had the friends I had. It wasn't long before I lost my job working at the bar, and I would begin to experience money struggles, but the bank I had a mortgage with would always provide me with a loan without issue. It was madness how easy they provided me with loans. I got a £5,000 loan and would again be on my feet without a care in the world.

Chapter Seven

New Years Eve

I was approached and offered a role as a doorman in Speke. I was offered £60 per night and thought it good money, as I would have my drinks paid for when going out afterwards. I would be doing the door with my mates, so I felt safe and okay, even though I didn't like some of the local lads around the area. I had become friends with a girl who I met in Liverpool, she was from Speke, nothing happened between us, we were just good friends. I would pop to her mums and her mum would laugh at me, calling me nuts, due to the silly situations I had got myself in. Her mum would often call me a lovely lad and a lad who was hanging out with the wrong bunch. I knew I possessed intelligence; due to the job roles I had achieved. When I managed the supermarket, I completed that role with success, and I was a well-liked person. I had many good qualities, but I just wasn't using them correctly and it was a shame, as I was a wasted talent in a way. Working as a doorman was going okay, it was a good way to socialise, I guess. It was leading up to New Years eve 2000, and this was a big new year's eve for everyone throughout the world. There was tension in the air that week, as it was clear that the war was still going on between doormen and the landlords. Some of my friends at the time were wearing bullet proof vests. I thought that was crazy and not needed. It just didn't seem possible for people to shoot at others, not around a few local pubs anyway. I foolishly believed that only happened in the movies.

My friend at Speke told me that she thought it was mad for me to be doing the door, her mum also stated that I should not be doing it. The week leading up to new year's eve, and up to this point, working as a doorman was going okay, but a few friends visited me at Penketh. We discussed New Years eve and how to have to be extra cautious, then, for the first time, I started to become slightly nervous with the role as a doorman in that area. I went out for drinks at a Liverpool nightclub a few days before New Years eve and during that evening I met a girl, she was German, and I arranged to see her New Years eve for a few drinks after I had finished working.

New year's eve was finally here, and all seemed okay. I was standing mostly outside talking to people entering the pub. I stood next to the landlord, but little did I know that people were planning to kill him that very evening. I stood looking around, and for a few moments, I felt strange, and I began to daydream about life in general. I suddenly heard loud crackling noises that resembled firecrackers. I didn't realise or even feel the first bullet hit me. It entered my stomach and exited my back. It is crazy to think one can't feel a bullet ripping through their body. The body is an amazing machine, I clearly went into some form of shock. I then felt my arm being dragged, and as I turned, I felt like I was hit by a car. The impact to my waist and leg area was extreme. I genuinely thought a car had driven into the doorway. The second bullet caused most damage, badly damaging my hip and femur. I flew to the ground and hit the floor hard. I was then dragged into the pub by a mate who was also a doorman that night, but as I was being dragged a third bullet hit my left foot and travelled up my leg. I was thrown to the floor out the way.

I ended up laying against a barstool, which must have fell over, as it was positioned on its side, which was perfect for me to lay against. It seemed like a lifetime before the police entered the pub and cleared the area. The police entered the pub like the SAS that evening, which wouldn't have looked out of place, as the pub was like a war zone. I was told over fifty bullets was fired into the pub doorway that night. The police have fantastic forensics, as they mapped the route of every bullet fired, which is remarkable that such a thing is even possible. My mate from Runcorn was also badly hit and very lucky, as a bullet that hit him only just missing his bowel. I believe he has suffered with a chest muscle since the shooting. I will never forget how this mate and his brother came to see me at hospital, these were good lads; it is sad in a way that we have not seen each other for many years now. I did see the older brother whilst watching my son play football many years later. It was nice seeing him, and it brought back many memories seeing his face. I instantly pictured how he would come to see me and his brother. I can still picture every moment from the night of the shooting, and when looking back, even now, I start to get butterflies in my chest and become slightly nervous. I guess it is the body remembering the trauma. Without knowing, still to this very day, I always sit facing the doorway. My counsellor stated that's so that I have a clear view of the entrance door, so I know that I have an escape route. I forget I do it now, but occasionally I will wonder why I sit were I do when entering a restaurant or pub. I guess the memory of trauma will live with me forever. After my operation I was placed into the intensive care unit, and high independence unit afterwards, it was very tough in them units. There was a male nurse who was very feminine.

He was so nasty and seemed to drag me when cleaning the sheets, I told him it hurt and he would say, 'shut up.' I was angry inside but had no energy or ability to argue. I remember becoming more aware of my surroundings. This was not until weeks after I came out from the operation. I remember asking a nurse what date it was, and she replied something like the 6th of January. This meant I was in hospital for my birthday and as I became more aware of my surroundings, I remembered the issue with my leg. I immediately reached out and grabbed my leg. I began crying as I realised my leg had been saved. I had no feeling in my right leg at all, but I was just happy that it was still there.

I shouted out to the nurse with joy, that I still have my leg. The nurse came over to me and explained that I have my leg, yes, but I may not have full use of it, as the sciatic nerve and other nerves were badly damaged. It is a case of waiting and hoping. The physiotherapist came to visit me and gave me exercises. These were very minimum, such as moving my toes. I did everything she asked and ten times more. I would be awake at 2 a.m. doing the exercises for hours, as I couldn't bear the thought of not having the full use of my leg. My parents came to visit me whilst I lay in the bed, and during his time, I was still being given blood. The drip was feeding blood into my arm, I also had a caveator attached to my bladder, I was still in a bad way. My mum leaned over me saying, 'You are going to lose your house lad, we cannot pay the bills and won't be able to save it, you're losing everything am afraid, lad' This was the last thing I needed to hear, as I was in such a state. It was yet again selfish behaviour of my mum. It was sickening to be saying such a thing to someone who was lying in such a state. The NHS provided a counsellor for me who explained I will suffer PTSD and have other issues for a long time to come.

She was explaining how I may have to deal with a disability in my right leg. She was very nice and understanding. She demonstrated much patience with me, as I was upset at the thought of not walking as I once did. The councillor told me she was concerned with how my mum was towards me, and she ordered for my mum to leave on one occasion. My parents caused more harm than good when it came to my mental health. The abuse they inflicted continued into adulthood. My parents visited me regularly and I dreaded it at times. They even told me how they have rooted through my house and looked at everything I owned. It was a horrible feeling knowing that someone had been at your home rooting. Having my mum's family visit was the nicest part.

My grandparents visited me and each time they sat beside my bed I would feel at complete ease. I would see a few of my aunties, and my favourite auntie who was obsessed with Elvis. I still think back how I would spend hours in her room being told everything there was to know about Elvis. She would even quiz me with questions about Elvis and stated that I should know this one as we had talked the previous day about it. All my uncles and aunties were there, and this made me feel safe and loved. Their approach was very different to that of my parents. My extended family are loving and caring people. It makes me very angry and upset the way my parents would slag off the family at times and make us dislike them in a way. I would then call my family as that was what I was taught to do. My mother would make up with the family and then turn on me for calling them, It was constant mental and physical abuse. I regret ever saying a bad word about my family. They are good people and have in the past cared a lot for me, and clearly loved me.

I was offered a private room, but I turned it down as I wanted to be near people, even if they were all old. Ninety percent of the people on my ward were all pensioners. Most needed to be in a care home and not in the hospital taking up the beds, It was wrong, as many people were left in the corridor having to wait due to no beds. I remember asking a nurse to put me in a corridor, so a patient could have my space. The nurse didn't allow it due to the state I was still in. Friends and other doormen would all come in to see me. I was handed money on two occasions, and I would have a nurse place horse racing bets for me as a way of entertaining myself. A couple of my mates from Bootle popped in to see me and were laughing, asking me why I was doing the door in Speke. One close friend came in to see me, he is a huge guy, around 6ft 4 and had been a previous heavyweight boxer, who did well when boxing, had an okay record I was told. I think he once boxed in the army. He went on for an hour telling me that, most of these lads doing the doors these days are idiots and far from tough. They take a few steroids and think that makes them tough when it doesn't.

He was telling me that these mugs who brag about being shot or stabbed were all losers and dickheads, that they had watched way too many gangster movies. He went onto say, 'who works for £60 a night?' stating he wouldn't get out of bed for that. He named a few bars and areas around Liverpool, telling me that the doorman only works those doors to look tough and act hard, and only mostly pick on kids to show off. He was right and I guess doormen are very different now than that of the old school lads. I went out around Warrington recently, which was very rare for me, as I dislike the place and saw those typical type doormen on that night out.

Trying their best to look tough when the facts are, they work for very little money and are far from tough. One guy on that night out was kissing a girl at the doorway, she appeared to work at the bar. I walked in and said, 'alright mate' and smiled. He just frowned at me for no reason whatsoever when I was being polite and nice. These are the types that are not wanted in town centres for me, and it is them who cause the trouble at times. I find them embarrassing, but don't get me wrong, not all doormen are like that, as around Liverpool, as an example, there are many decent lads working the doors. I know a fair few who are decent lads and would never cause trouble and certainly don't walk round trying to prove a point.

I was starting to become a lot more aware now that blood was not needed as much, but some of the medication, such as morphine, was stopping me from thinking clear. Two police officers from Liverpool CID attended the hospital to get statements from me, and I agreed, even though my mum was telling them I wasn't well enough. I provided the statement, but they told me that they could not use the statement, as I was high on medication. Apparently, the statement was a bit mad, as I stated that I was hit with cannon balls from a nearby war ship. It is funny looking back when thinking about it. The D.I. visited me several times afterwards and would laugh when telling me what I told him at the hospital. He was a good officer and a decent guy. It was extremely interesting the time he spent with me, as he would tell me when he was under cover doing the door many years before, as well as many other stories. The hospital ward was never without incidents. Pensioners trying to escape or getting drunk in the night, as many would hide flasks of whisky in their trousers. I started more intense exercises, and I was told I would need to learn to walk again.

These were very scary and worrying times, as this was the time I would learn if I would ever walk properly again. I stood in a huge metal machine; it held my body weight. I was trying to move my legs, but the pain was severe. I began to make good progress, and the doctors were impressed. After a few more weeks I was told I could be discharged, but the physiotherapist disagreed. I was to stay at hospital for a few more weeks. The girl who I met in the run up to New Years eve began to visit me and would continue dating me. I needed this, as it was approaching the time that I would be informed if I would still have full use of my leg again. I was petrified at the thought of having a disabled leg, but the surgeon was very impressed with my progress. I was very determined and there was still lots of fight in me. The morning came where I would find out how well my leg had recovered. The surgeon stated that I will have use of my leg, but they will not know for many months whether I would drag it or not. In the days leading up to my discharge I needed to have tubes removed that ran through my body from the entry and exit wound. A young nurse who was still not yet qualified came to my bed. I could see she didn't read the notes fully, and clearly not reading or noticing that the tubes were stitched in at the front and rear of my body she unclipped the stitches at the front entry wound, but not at the rear. She began pulling hard, blood was seeping out of the front and rear. The pain was immense, and I started to pass out before the man in the next bed told the nurse to stop and get help. A ward manager came along and informed me that the tube has been pulled into the body, as it is still connected to stitches and that they will need to go inside and unclip the stitches somehow. I cannot begin to describe the pain I went through that day.

It was finally coming up to the day that I would be discharged. The counsellor attended my bed whilst my father listened. I was told that I may suffer panic attacks when leaving the hospital and for my parents to take things slow with me. I was wheeled out in a wheelchair, as I could still not stand on my own, my father put me in the passenger seat of his car, it was just me and him. He was very cruel that day, he was laughing and pointing to the roof saying that someone was trying to get me. I was shaking inside and began panicking. I got home to my parents and was provided with the small fourth bedroom., This was the room next to my youngest brother's room. Each evening before going to sleep he would tap on the wall, and I would tap back. It was our way of saying goodnight to each other, but later in life he admitted that he tapped on the wall to make sure I was still alive. He told me this at my father's hospital beside. The days leading up to my father's passing, January 2023.

Nurses had to attend my parents' home each day to clean out my wounds. This was a painful experience, as they would have to clean inside the exit and entry holes that were still, even during that time, slightly open. My parents would often ask me, what do I plan to do for work and how will I pay my bills. I didn't need to think about any of that during that time due to the state I was in. I was never given a moments peace due to my parents, even during these very concerning times. I was more worried if my leg would recover fully and how my state of mind would cope over the coming months. My girlfriend would visit my parents' home and make her way up to my bedroom and comfort me. She would say that I needed to escape my mums due to how my parents were towards me. I would pray every night that my leg would fully recover.

I would continue reading the blue bible that I kept from my hospital bedside. It finally came to the week that I would leave my parents' home and go home to my house at Burtonwood, a house I was lucky to still have, as the bank applied for a repossession order due to no payments being made whilst I was in hospital. Thankfully, Shelter attended court on my behalf, stopping the repossession order that the bank had applied for. I did not have to pay any mortgage payments for a three-month period and after that it would be interest only for six months. This allowed me some breathing space. It allowed me to concentrate on my health and state of mind. The flash backs began to get severe, especially now that I was living alone. My home was facing a large field, and I felt isolated. I would often picture people with guns running through the fields towards my home. I would start crying with fear and hide in the loft. The loft was converted into a third bedroom, and I would often hide there of an evening, as I was convinced that someone was on the way to get me. I was called by the girl from Knotty Ash who I once dated, she had something to tell me. She met with me and was upset, She informed me that she had become pregnant with my baby but had an abortion whilst in Australia on holiday. She left and we never spoke again, I was left confused and couldn't really digest anything like that during that time, as the medication was strong, and my state of mind was not in the best of shape. I started to feel stronger, and my leg was recovering well. I started to move my foot with ease. It was clear I was fully recovering but was still due to attend the hospital for updates. The surgeon stated that he cannot explain how I have managed to fully recover to the extent I have and in such a short period.

I decided to not see any of my friends from Liverpool and I distanced myself from all friends. It was mainly my mates from Liverpool who I needed to distance from. However, the lads from Runcorn were all ok lads. My mate who was also shot was a decent lad, a lad who I grew very fond of. I liked his older brother too. The lads from Runcorn were of no harm, just decent lads. They were very different from my mates in Liverpool. Some mates from Liverpool were decent, they were tough and respected lads, but also decent. There was just a few I needed to distance myself from. I guess I just wanted this to be a whole new start for me. I started to go out on my own. I went into Liverpool on a Saturday night, but I was recognised instantly. People came over and invited me in the clubs and pubs offering me free drinks. I made my way to Slater street, Liverpool city centre, where an old friend from boxing was working as doorman. I began to spend time with him. I would have a drink in the club he worked and wait for him to finish. We would venture out into Liverpool for a few drinks at late-night clubs. I was not contacted by my old friends at all, and this was a good thing as I wanted a fresh start, and it was nice to be back friends with lads that I had known from a young age. One evening I attended a bar in the area where my friend was working and I was approached by a doorman, who took me to one side and asked me if I could get him a gun. I thought this was strange, people assumed because I was shot, I was dealing in guns. I walked away from him and told my friend what had happened. We followed that doorman home that night after he finished work. He drove to a house, entered it for a short time, then he came out leaving his car. He then walked around the corner to another car and then drove to another property approximately ten miles away.

My friend seemed to think he was working for the police. It seemed crazy to me; It was like a movie scene. The following week he approached me again. I told him straight that I do not sell guns and want no part in guns ether. I walked away from him and continued with my night out. My friend informed me that he was working the following week outside of town and that I could meet him there for a few drinks. I agreed, but whilst traveling on the M57 to meet him.

I received a call from the girl from Knotty Ash who wanted to meet with me again, I instantly turned the car around when I could and went in the opposite direction on the motorway to meet with her. We spoke about if we could start seeing each other again, but I was unaware just how mentally unwell I was at that time. I was carrying on with life as though all was okay, but little did I realise that inside I was extremely unwell, and this would become more apparent as time passed by. I didn't hear from my friend for several weeks, and then unexpectedly I was called with the news that my friend had also been shot whilst working as a doorman. I was informed the hospital he was staying at and began visiting him. I couldn't believe that if I didn't turn around that evening to go and meet the girl, I may have been involved in a shooting incident for the second time. I clearly wasn't learning and understanding that being around that nightlife was dangerous. If you go somewhere, where you are likely to get into trouble and you get into trouble, then it is your own fault. This statement my father made would ring around in my head constantly. I fell out with the girl from Knotty Ash, she became upset that I was not treating her nice or committing to her. I was just very unwell at the time; I received a call from her uncle who was also a doorman in Liverpool. He was shouting down the phone, so I called the police as I began to panic.

I had no idea why I panicked; I just did. I didn't do anything bad to the girl, I mean, I had not hit her or anything, I was just not committing to her. I was not able to commit to anything during this time. I was at home when calling the police, but they told me to go to a nearby pub or public place. I went to a nearby pub at Burtonwood and ordered a pint. I started to talk to the staff and made them aware I just moved into the area from Liverpool, when out the blue police stormed into the pub, and wrapped a large coat around me and bundled me into a BMW car and pulled away at speed. They took me to a police station and had me under protective custody. They questioned me about the threats made over the phone and informed me that because I had been involved in a recent shooting, they had to respond in such a manner. It was a very scary experience, especially the speed the officer drove the BMW. The police informed me that they had visited the persons house who I argued with and there was nothing for me to worry about. I continued with life but would often get upset knowing I had ruined a good chance with that girl. I continued with my recovery and would walk as much as possible. I would leave the house for hours at a time, pushing myself as much as possible. My legs began to get their strength back and before I knew it, I started jogging at a slow pace. The leg and foot didn't drag like I dreaded. My body was healing nicely and all getting back to normal, but my mind was suffering badly. The flash backs and anxiety were getting worse and worse. I needed help and attended group therapy sessions that I was referred to by my GP. I was informed that after completing the course that they could not help me. I started to attend more intense one on one sessions, that also didn't really help me fully. I knew that this would be a time thing. I needed to accept that this may take years for me to get over it all. My body recovered well, and I started to look at what activities

I could take part in, so I volunteered to coach a local football team. My brother played for the team, and he loved the fact that I was the coach. My dad didn't ever attend, and this was because I was the coach I feel, it was a shame as my brother was brilliant and it was him who brought winning ways to a team, a team that had not won a game for a while. I completed my FA coaching badges, and I started to feel that life was turning around for me, as I was now mixing amongst good working professional people. All the parents were lovely and the young lads who played on the team were a brilliant bunch. I began to look at my sales ability and thought how best to use such. I applied for sales roles in transport and managed to gain a role as a development manager. The role paid well, and it came with a company car. This could be the start I needed and the start that could get me a career, most of all, it would get me away from town centres and the nightlife that I seemed to be addicted too. I started work at Appleton Thorn industrial estate for an Irish transport company. The owner started teaching me how to quote transport. He was teaching me well and within a few weeks I could look at any items and price it up just from viewing the item. Many other salesmen would need tape measures, but I soon developed a natural ability in viewing items, knowing the sizes and cost it would be to ship such. This was a great ability to possess, as I could quote at speed and win the business easier. Many salesmen would stand around for an hour measuring without really engaging with the clients. I walk into a warehouse instantly know the cost and began talking about the weather and football. I would become friends with the clients and build a relationship at speed. This was very beneficial to me personally, as if I ever left a company the people would want to follow me. I would then be able to demand a certain pay wage, as I would be bringing work along with me. I quickly realised this and knew I had a chance of gaining employment with a high salary. I was getting along well with my new role, but my mental health would start affecting my work. I would start crying for no reason at all or start to feel nervous if I heard loud noises. I would come home alone and get bored at speed, so I would start going out to Warrington town centre on my own. There were a few doormen who recognised me from Liverpool and would allow me to get in the club for free. They knew who I was friends with and would often ask about my friends. I didn't want to make anyone aware that I distanced myself from such friends, as I was getting free drinks and free entry to the club. I was also recognised one evening by an off-duty police officer, who approached me and invited me on a night out. I was now out with around nine off duty police officers who behaved worse than my mates from Liverpool. I was shocked how they were that night and was more shocked when a doormen came at me, as good as threatening me because his girlfriend fancied me apparently. The off-duty police officer took the doormen to one side and threatened him. He came back to me, and I asked what he said to him, he replied 'I told him I will plant shit in his car, and to never go near you again.' I couldn't believe my ears, maybe he was just drunk that night and saying silly things, after all, we are all only human. I never went out with the police officers again after that, even though one or two contacted me to go out with them. I just felt uncomfortable going near that scene in nightclubs. I gave the clubs and night life a break for a few weeks and instead just kept myself to myself. I would often just walk for hours in the rain. I would picture what life may be like in the future if meeting a girl and getting married. The thought of having children made me feel happy and it would be a dream come true for me. I noticed that by daydreaming a lot, it helped me divert my mind from thinking thoughts that would cause anxiety. I would often think that people were coming to get me or have flashbacks about the night I was shot, but if I were watching a movie; let's say a spy movie, and then go for a walk afterwards, I would picture myself as a spy and imagine people following me in cars. I would develop this whole role play in my mind. It sounds crazy, but it helped me divert thoughts about the shooting and It helped calm my anxiety. I would always have trouble sleeping when at the house at Burtonwood on my own. I would lay awake until 4 a.m. I noticed I would constantly check the windows and doors to make sure they were locked. No matter how many times I checked the doors, I would still go back an hour later and check the doors once more, It was draining at times. I had split up with my girlfriend and at this stage of my life, I was mostly always on my own at home. I had Sky TV, but no Sky channels, as I cancelled my subscription. I kept the Sky TV box, and I noticed that the channel TCM was free. I would sit for hours watching old black and white movies. I was starting to feel very isolated living at Burtonwood. Sometimes, I would get a hotel in Liverpool just to escape the isolation. I left work for a six-week period as I was unwell. I suffered a few panic attacks, and I decided to go live in a hotel at the Liverpool docks. The world cup was on during that time, so it was a great atmosphere around town. All the pubs had the football games on, and I would place a small football coupon bet for excitement, Whilst I lived at the hotel, I would feel safe, as no one could possibly know I was staying there. I became friends with strangers and people who stood at the Albert dock admiring the view. I would walk over to them and just start talking. The next minute I would pop for a pint with a few, it was okay living at the hotel, as I was not recognised when popping into Liverpool. I was glad not seeing any old friends, as I didn't want to go back to that nightlife full of clubs and late nights. I began running of a morning and getting my fitness back. The fitness helped with my state of mind. I starting to feel mentally strong, but every other week an incident would occur. A loud noise of a passing car or bang of a car door. These little things would send me into a state of panic. I began to realise I was still unwell and dreaded the thought that I may be like this for many years to come. I began reading a lot, and read up on PTSD, with how people suffer who had been shot. I became scared, as some stories stated that the victims suffered forever. Money was okay due to what I earned from a well-paid job. I managed to save money too, as my mortgage was a very low rate at that time. I was finally given my criminal injuries compensation. My dad had his solicitor friend manage it. He managed it badly, as I was handed just £5,000 for my injuries. This was nothing compared to what I went through and how I was still suffering. My dad was a hard worker and always provided. He was a success, but when it came to business and business ventures, he was far from great. Many people who my dad dealt with took advantage of him, and I was now being taken advantage of in the way of a poor pay out. Other legal advisers later stated they could have got me much more. I should never have taken my dad's advice with where to go. His solicitor friend would have made good money with legal fees, and at my expense, as stated my dad was not the best at certain advice. When he retired, he bought a pest control franchise business, and lost thousands in the deal. This would be a regular occurrence with my dad. He was great at life advice in avoiding trouble, but terrible with mortgage advice and business advice. I returned to my home and became instantly bored. I missed being at Liverpool, and a lot more after my happy hotel experience. My father called me out of the blue stating that I still owed him money from when I was in hospital. I had money, but I was far from comfortable. I was shocked that he wanted the money, it was around £800 he stated from paying a few of my bills, but I question that my parents spent that amount. I was at home that week when having this chat with my parents about money, and it was the week that I did the lottery for the first time. I was at the local Asda and decided to pick a few random numbers. I went home and I got the first five numbers that Saturday night. I was jumping for joy, but in the end, I only won £2,700. It was ridiculous you get that much for five numbers, but millions for six. I was handed a cheque for the lottery win and when it cleared, I drove straight to my dad's shop and handed him £800 cash. He said, 'thank you,' but looking back I am disgusted he took it from me, especially when he was doing so well in life with all the shops he owned. He knew I was still recovering from a terrible incident and struggling. If it were my son, I would only ever help him and not force him to pay back money from when he was in hospital. I still question that they ever paid any of the bills, as they were always very tight and not ones for giving me help when it was needed. I may be wrong, but it's just how I have been made to feel.

Chapter Eight

The Road To Paris

I went back to the Liverpool hotel with some of my winnings from the lottery but didn't stay as long this time, and soon made my way back to Burtonwood. I sat at home and didn't panic as I had £5,000 in the bank and my mortgage was only £300 a month, so there was no panic for me to get work. I got bored and applied for a credit card with my mortgage company, Northern Rock. They handed me a £10,000 credit card with ease. I was totally shocked at this. They also provided me with a £5,000 loan. They did not apply a charge on my home and all loans were unsecured. It was as though they were handing out free money. I started to go out a lot and noticed that when I suffered panic attacks or anxiety, I could calm the symptoms by placing a few bets on horses as it would take my mind off the anxiety and put me in a calm and excited frame of mind. Little did I know that at the same time I was building up an addiction to gambling. This was not the first time I suffered with gambling, as I suffered when age 17. I returned from the army and would often bet without thinking anything of it. My parents once went to work, and I found bundles of cash hidden under the floorboards in the bathroom area and in video covers in the loft. It was obviously my father's money, but I have no idea why that money was there and still don't know why today. I took £200 and went betting. I lost and I came home crying in panic, it was no shock I was addicted to gambling, as my dad would often take me into a betting office when age six plus.

We would go home and watch the horses. He would also take me into betting officers whilst his friend, Bob, placed bets. I was asked to hand cash to the cashier, and this was at the age of around eight. I called my parents at work and told them I had taken £200 and that I wanted to kill myself. My mum went off the phone and spoke to my dad, she came back and told me that my dad had agreed and told me to go kill myself. I was scared about the thought of them getting home, even though I promised that I would pay the money back. This time it was different, as this money was mine and money I needed, as I lived alone now. I needed to learn to manage my money in a safe and sensible manner. I started to go out again and one Saturday evening whilst at Mr Smith's nightclub I spotted an attractive blonde standing with her friends. I approached her, asking her out on a date. We exchanged numbers and began texting for several weeks. I was aware from other sources that she had recently been treated badly by an ex-boyfriend and that she was still in touch with him. I didn't care and agreed to meet on the date. We met and spoke for a while before agreeing to go back to my home for a coffee. We got on well and I took an instant attraction to her. I felt safe that someone was with me in the house, and she started to stay at my home daily. Within less than two months she became pregnant. We decided to live together and started to plan a future. We both agreed that we wanted to move from Burtonwood, as the neighbours were a nightmare. The next-door neighbour would block our car daily. We enjoyed our time there overall, as we would go out on daily walks in the area. One happy memory I have is when out walking during bonfire night we came across a large field and there was a fire still burning away. There was not a person in sight, and we stood enjoying the fire to ourselves.

We went on a few little holidays together. Including visiting my parents' caravan at Abasoch. We went on one little adventure and ended up lost in the countryside. We finally came across a pub and popped in for a few drinks, it was like a scene from the American Werewolf in London movie, as everyone turned around and looked at us. When leaving the pub, we took a long walk back to the caravan to meet my parents. I still have a few pictures of those weekend' breaks. It was made clear that the baby would not be born at Burtonwood. When my partner went into labour the car was blocked in yet again, and we had to drive into the field to get out. It was already known that we had a little girl on the way from the scan, and I wanted the baby to be named. We named our daughter, and I would begin singing, Over the Rainbow, whilst resting my head on my partner's stomach. I was so excited for the birth. My daughter was born a healthy weight of near 9llb. This was the happiest moment of my life; I literally couldn't get over it. I would constantly be holding my daughter and was so very proud to be a father. We had to move from Burtonwood, as the neighbours were becoming worse and worse and I didn't want to be arrested for fighting with them, especially not now being a father. Thankfully, the house sold at speed, and we moved away to the far side of Warrington. The house we rented was tiny, but we made it a home. I was earning good money at work and my partner was also getting on well in her job role at work. Little did she know that I was struggling badly, I would often cry in my car for no reason. I went to my GP to gain help and advice and was referred to a counsellor once more. I was informed that I was not ready for all the responsibility just yet, and that it will have a negative impact. The counsellor explained that the shooting incident was still fresh and recent. I was still not well and struggling badly and more than I realised. The counselling continued for nine months.

My partner became pregnant straight away with our second child. There was just twelve months between our first child and our second. We were to have a boy this time around, and he too was a healthy weight at just over 9llb. We were blessed with healthy children. I was the happiest man alive and couldn't believe I was so lucky to be a father of two perfect children. I had a few months break from counselling and tried to continue with life as normal. I struggled constantly, as I was always up and down. I would become angry for no reason and couldn't control it. I even pushed my partner back whilst she was pregnant with our second child. I can't put it into words how much I hate myself looking back knowing I pushed someone who I loved and who was carrying my child at the time. This was an isolated incident when it came to physical abuse, but I was also verbally abusive at times. I would drive to work crying uncontrollably, hating myself. I had a meeting early one morning with my PA afterwards I set off on the M6 to my first meeting of the day, all was ok that morning, but thirty minutes into the drive, I started crying for no reason. I pulled over and couldn't drive no more, I even started to walk away from the car and walked to the nearest junction before turning around and making my way back to the car. I drove straight back to work and handed my keys in, informing the director that I was resigning. He looked at me concerned and told me to take the car home and that he would call me in a few days. He called and asked how I was, asking if I was ready to come back to work, I agreed and went back to work. It was a constant battle, and it affected me in so many ways. I was unwell, but a lot more unwell than I realised at that time. My partner didn't really support me with what I was going through, but looking back, why should she, how could she possibly understand any of it. I started counselling once more and the therapist informed me that she wanted my partner to attend with me, so she could explain to her what I was going through. The therapist stated that it was of real importance that my partner understood how my illness was affecting me. I went home and asked if she would attend, and she declined saying, 'It isn't my issue, and I am not going.' I accepted her wishes and continued with life. I was gambling more and more. The equity from the house sale was in my bank account.

I gambled over £18,000 in a six-week period, with the largest bet being a £7,000 win on one horse, which got beat in a photo finish. The gambling gave me a rush and it was deflecting my anxiety and other PTSD issues. I just wasn't aware that it was creating other issues, as an addiction to gambling is not a great thing, especially when one has two young children to provide for. I hated renting too, as the landlady was a vile person. She would make me count the money very slow, accepting only cash. We began to look for a home to buy this time, as we got accepted for a mortgage. I still had some of the money left over from the first house sale. We found a large three-bedroom semi-detached home 5 miles outside Warrington, in another part of Cheshire, but the property needed much work. It was up for sale for £140,000. I put an offer forward of £125,000 and it was accepted at speed. We were out at Chester zoo that day and I said to my partner, 'If she has accepted at that speed, it makes me think that she will take less.' I called the agents back up and stated that I can only get a mortgage for £120,000. The phone didn't ring for an hour, which made me think it was declined, but it was great news, as the offer was accepted. We moved into our own home together and the children appeared excited and happy running around. The first few months went okay, but my struggles continued. I began drinking heavily and continued to gamble on a weekly basis. I neglected my duties as a husband, and I was not motivated to carry out the most simply of duties. I wouldn't sleep with my partner for long periods, and this caused frustration. I had a meeting one afternoon with an attractive young female who was flirting with me. I went back to her apartment after work, and we ended up on her couch. I got naked and we began kissing. However, I pushed her off me and told her I couldn't do it, and I went home upset, hating myself for getting into that position. The female continued to call my work wanting to speak to me. However, my PA told her that I had a partner and to not call again. I didn't even know that my PA said this until a month after it happened. It was just an escape, I guess, meeting with that female. We had meetings at the Trafford centre and even went for a walk in Altringham. We only kissed once during the apartment experience, and I stopped it that night. I was unwell and didn't know what I was doing half the time. People always state that mental illness is used an excuse when committing wrongful acts, but a lot of the time, sadly, *it is* down to mental health.

I was very unwell and suffering badly with PTSD. I had been for a few years at this point and things appeared to be getting worse and not better. I was taking anti-depressants and drinking whilst taking such medication. I had no control over my moods or behaviour, and I would be sad almost daily, but hid the sadness as much as possible. I was embarrassed when crying, so I would hide or go for a drive when I needed to cry. Crying was a way of letting it all out, after a good cry, I would feel slightly better for a few hours. It was now time to start thinking about marriage, so I booked a table at the Pan Am bar in Liverpool. We were the only people on the top floor. The staff brought over a large bouquet of flowers, and I got on one knee and asked her to marry me. I purchased a 2.2 carat diamond, which was the most expensive ring I could afford at the time. She said, 'yes', and that evening was amazing, even if my partner did say immediately after saying yes, 'I thought you was going to propose at the top of the Eiffel tower?' I gave the staff a good tip and we went home happy. The next chapter of our lives was making wedding arrangements, and this can be very stressful. We both agreed on the venue at speed. The Statham Lodge at Lymm was a beautiful venue and it had links to my partner's family, as her grandfather would visit when it was a casino I believe. I continued to earn good money and was earning more than my partner realised, but I would constantly gamble. I would always make sure all the bills were paid and whatever was left over I would gamble away, it seemed okay with me, as I told myself that I had paid all the bills and therefore I was a good providing husband and father, but little did I realise at the time that I was slowing us down with progressing and building in life, as the money I was earning could have probably got us a larger house and many more holidays. Family life was happy overall, and we tried to give our children the most normal upbringing as possible. I would climb on the extension roof each Christmas Eve dressed as Santa, handing presents to my children. I would pass down presents and the children would smile with excitement. We still have pictures and videos on those evenings. My most favourite time with my children was walking them to school. I would do this daily, and on the way, I would make up stories, one being, the boy with the magic coin. My children would leave school and ask me what happened next. I miss those days so much and wish that they would have lasted forever, sadly, in the blink of an eye the children became adults. The second incident took place in the home. I stated that I didn't love my partner and wanted to split up. She stood up and as she left the house she spat in my face. I kicked out the very moment she did that, and my foot connected with her backside. She got in her car upset and drove around the corner, waiting.

This was the second time I had placed my hands on my partner, yes, a foot to the backside is still a serious assault. It was being spat at, I guess, it just seemed to trigger my instant reaction. It is a horrible thing when someone spits in your face. I was causing all the issues, and causing the arguments, it was me who was the root of the issue. I was very unwell and felt trapped in my life. I loved my children more than life; I was just very unwell. I reached out and got in touch with an old school friend, Steven. When we were at school we weren't allowed in the same class, as we would instantly start laughing while looking at each other. My desk would be placed outside, and I would look through the classroom window and make Steven laugh. We bunked off school every other day and we would pretend to be filming documentaries, which is ironic, as Steven developed a passion for film making when he left school. Steven was the most talented lad I knew; he sadly suffered a bit of bullying from the odd few individuals who attended our school. One bully who targeted Steven also made an aim for me, but once outside my uncles in Huyton. I battered that bully in front of his mates, and he didn't try it on with me again. I helped Steven at times with how he was bullied. I stuck up for him as a good friend should do. When we left school, I didn't see Steven for many years, but once I settled with my new family, I decided to contact him. I would often skive from work, as I managed my own time, so it was like the good old days. I would pick Steven up from his parents' home and we would go out for the day. Meeting up with Steven was an escape for me, it took me back to my childhood. I remember sitting in Steven's house as a young lad one afternoon talking to his dad about football and his dad became angry as Steven was laughing, so his dad threw him out the house and continued to chat with me about football. Steven then appeared in the living room window, laughing, we had such a laugh.

I brought Steven to my home, and he met my children and partner. He stayed the night on the couch, but sadly, June 2024. I noticed on Instagram that his sister had posted that he had passed away. I had not seen Steven for many years at that point, as we fell out over something that I caused. I introduced him to a terrible person, who sadly became his partner for a while, I was told that she treated him badly. I felt partly responsible, as it was me who introduced them to each other. I believe it was her who kept me and Steven apart for all those years before he passed. I cried the night I found out that Steven had passed, and for several days after that. Steven was so very talented, and he deserved so much more from life, He went far too young. I should have had him at my wedding, but Steven lived in America during that time. He created a 3D image of the Liverpool Overhead Railway and created some amazing things that I hope will live on and one day get noticed. I will always miss him and always look back laughing at the times we had together. I still talk to him when I am feeling down, as he is the one friend who never failed at making me laugh. The wedding was fast approaching. Some of my mum's family didn't attend as we fell out. This was yet again down to my upbringing and how we were taught to hate family members by my mum, but when she made up with them, we were left disliked by the family for the wrongful statements I had made. I regret ever saying anything bad about my extended family, as they are all lovely and amazing people. Looking back, I have a lot of anger towards my mum for the way she made me think about them at times. The wedding went well, my partner's sister attended who I like very much, she is such a lovely person, and her parents, who are both amazing people. Our honeymoon was in Paris, and it was a lovely break, despite the fact I was full of a cold. I continued to work, but I was jumping from job to job again. I finally got a role at Target Ireland; this was a very well-paid role. I would oversee the northwest areas, and spent over two years in this role, before being made redundant. I was very fortunate to be head hunted by an Irish rival company, who offered me a role with even more money. I was fast tracked to a senior position overlooking over a hundred staff. This role went well, as I managed my own time, but after three years I would be made redundant again due to the company closing. I was offered several jobs in Ireland, but it meant me having to live there. I sat at home and began to struggle with my mental illness again, and almost daily. We went on a mini break to Cornwall, but during our time there I had a severe panic attack, I remember laying down asking my wife to call ambulance, as I thought I was having a heart attack. She didn't seem concerned and instead casually asked me, 'you sure you just don't want some Gaviscon?' I couldn't believe my ears and tried calling 999 myself. The ambulance arrived and it was concluded that I suffered a panic attack. I felt embarrassed and left the ambulance red faced looking around at people looking at me. My in laws began to lend us money towards everyday shopping and I embarrassingly accepted, and I even began to ask to loan some money at times. We were struggling and not used to this way of life. I had been well paid for many years, so it was a shock with having to cut back. I did want to give the in-laws money when I separated with my wife, but the divorce and the costs my wife and her solicitor created during the time we ended our marriage made it impossible for me to pay anything. Looking back at the time we were married and struggling, I was constantly sat at home unsure how to make my life right again, and how I could become a better man. I lay on the couch one afternoon and sensed that my wife had something to tell me.

She looked at me smiling and I instantly knew that she was pregnant. I was so happy, I would have loads of children without a care as to how I would provide for them. Family is greatest blessing anyone would wish for.

Wedding venue, Statham Lodge, Lymm.

Chapter Nine

Hell

I needed to start thinking how to get out of the hole I was in. I wasn't working right now, but I did have money saved from my last job role. We went on holiday whilst my wife was pregnant. We went to France for the best holiday to date, and it was not unusual for my wife to arrange the holiday, as she was always brilliant at organising things. We had still not named our third child, but we knew he was a boy from the scans. I feel it's always best finding out if the baby is a boy or girl, as you can then start referring to the baby by name. We visited Lyon during our holiday to France and managed to check into a hotel, which was lucky as we had nothing pre-booked. They offered us the best room they had, but stated that the hotel was being decorated, but we would get a discounted price. The total cost was just £50 per night instead of the usual £300. It was an amazing large room with French doors overlooking the yard outside. There was a man playing a violin and lots of people walking by, we loved the hotel. One day whilst walking up to a huge hill towards a large cathedral looking building, I named my son. His name came to me during the walk, it was as clear as day. I even pictured my son's face; his name relates to our stay at Lyon. This would make the city a special place to us for the rest of our lives. My wife wasn't sure, and my mother-in-law didn't like the name at first, but it stuck, and soon all the family grew to like the name. He was a healthy baby, at a weight of 10lb. He was a very long baby, and I held him with so much love. I cannot put it into words how much I love my children; they are all a blessing. Sadly, for my youngest when he was just two years old, my wife came home as I lay in bed with him and informed me that she wanted a divorce. It was the 14th of February, Valentine's Day. She told me she had a house already arranged and had a moving in date. My first thought was about the kids, My daughter took it badly and wrote in a book that I found years later, 'Please Lord help me, as my parents are divorcing.' My eldest son, who I told in my van as we drove started crying. This was a terrible time for us all. For me, anyone who divorces lets their kids down. We all owe a duty to our children when we have them. We should not have kids unless we are certain of our love for our partner. It all sounds too much, and I guess that statement is far-fetched and unrealistic, but I just feel that one should try absolutely everything before giving up. Back in the day, people would not divorce with the ease that they do today. That is the issue with society I feel, people divorce far too easily today. I let my kids down, my wife let them down too, but I was felt more to blame due to my struggles. My body had always recovered well, but my mind was a right mess. PTSD had affected me for over ten years. It was the cause of me gambling thousands, ruining my marriage, and destroying the family environment that my children had at home. I wrote down on paper and asked my wife what she wanted money wise and what she wanted from the house. I couldn't let the house go, as this was the children's home and the only home they knew. I would never allow the house to be sold or be taken from me or the children. We agreed on a sum of money. I began taking all the items she requested from the house to her new home in my van. I gave her the sofa set, drawers, everything she wanted.

Most importantly, we agreed that I would have shared access with the kids. I accepted it all and immediately got to working on a plan of action in getting her and my kids back home. During this time, my father sold his business and retired. He was left with a van that he didn't need and gave it to me as a way of me creating an income with it. It was only worth around £1,500, but a good van all the same. I decided to set up a landscaping business. I remember once working on the queen's estate and learning gardening during my time living in Stoke. I loved it. I also remember working with my granddad at my grandparents' home. I had a natural love and ability for gardening. I got the side of the van printed up with a company name and secured a website address. I got thousands of leaflets printed and began spending hours each day posting leaflets. Before I knew it, my phone would start ringing, and I finally got my first job. It was at a girl's house on the Wirral, so it wasn't local.

I didn't realise that the girl had a thing for me, and I foolishly stayed at the house overnight. Nothing ever happened, as I made it very clear I didn't like her in that way. I finished the garden, and she became nasty with me because I didn't take her up on her advances. The girl had another female who lived with her, who worked for MI5. I was so fascinated with her work, but she wouldn't talk much about work, stating she wasn't allowed to talk on such matters. She knew martial arts and showed me moves, she obviously learnt via work I assume. I finished the work and never returned or kept in touch with the girl. She paid me just £600 for a huge patio and garden makeover, so I was taken advantage of in a way. I continued to post leaflets and finally got some local work. The first ever real job was a local client's home around the corner from my parents. She was a lovely customer, and it was a great experience working for her, she even gave me a tip at the end of the work. I took flowers around as a thank you. I made around £2,000 profit on this job and began to realise that I could create a little income from this work. I was fortunate to get another job straight away and earned £5,000 profit on it. I also won money from betting; it must have been approximately £4,000 that I won. I was now able to start paying my divorce settlement, but my wife wanted me to spend the money on holidays instead, so I did, thinking that it was a way of repairing the marriage. I spent near £20,000 on holidays and weekends away, from February 2014 up to late 2016. We would sleep in the same bed at some hotels, and I was convinced that the marriage was repairable. I mean, why wouldn't I if my wife was going away with me so much? I began to receive emails from what was clearly a fake account. The person was telling me that my wife had been having an affair at work. My wife told me to ignore it all, saying it was lies. My wife even asked me for a further £2,500 for a holiday that week, which I agreed to, and transferred the funds within a few days. I didn't know that at that time that my wife had applied for orders to restrict me going near her. I was finally told outright by the man's wife that my wife had been having an affair for the past few years. I was extremely upset and angry, but I didn't threaten anyone, nor smash or damage anything. I didn't assault anyone either, but I did send abusive text messages to my wife. I also shouted at my wife over the phone when the children could hear me. I didn't handle it well at all. I even went to the man's house to have a word with him, but he didn't answer. I finally spoke to him over the phone, and he was disrespectful. That call ended with him calling the police, making a statement of harassment. I admitted calling him and to my disgust I was arrested for two short telephone calls, which lasted a matter of minutes. I only wanted to know how long the affair had gone on for.

The way I was brought up in Huyton, you never went near a married woman and if a man approached you asking if you had an affair with his wife, you would be man enough to be open and tell the truth, especially if there are children involved. My wife applied for a non-molestation order due to the abusive text messages and calls I committed. Her solicitor came to my home and didn't even introduce himself. He simply asked me who I was and threw papers at my doorway, some of which hit me in my face. The papers instantly blew in the wind, all over the public road. I chased the man down the road. He was a tall man, approximately 6ft 4. I didn't care, as I was not allowing anyone to come to my door and assault me with paper. I forgot to realise as I chased him that I had only a towel around my waist, as I had just got out the shower, and as I ran the towel became loose and fell from me. I was now chasing a man whilst completely naked. I got back home after he sped away in a car. I picked up one of the papers and noticed my wife's name on it. I didn't understand what the papers were, so I went around to her house and asked if she knew what the papers were. She explained to me that it was an order preventing me to go near her. A week later whilst I was in the bath. The police came to my home and smashed my front door down, arresting me. I pleaded guilty to asking my wife what the papers were, which in turn, breached the orders. I was charged and sentenced to 120 community hours. I appealed and attended Crown court. The judge that day asked why I didn't plead not guilty to the breach, and I didn't know why, I was just in fear that was all. The judge asked me how many community hours I had completed at that stage. I stated, 'around 60'. He made an order that I didn't need to do anymore hours, but I must complete the rest of the probation. I only had a driving offence on my record at this stage, which occurred when I was just seventeen.

My wife's solicitor appeared obsessed with me, and to a worrying level. Her solicitor was sending me late night text messages, and some appeared to threaten me almost. My legal adviser who I instructed drafted a letter of concern about my wife's solicitor, I still have that letter today. My legal adviser stated that I should never have pleaded guilty, as the papers were not served correctly, and as a result, I had no idea what orders were in place. The approach by the police was sickening the day of the first arrest. They threatened to turn my house upside down if I didn't hand over my phone. I have no idea why they wanted my phone. I did complain and received an apology from an inspector who investigated the matter. I lost a lot of respect for the local police due to the handling of this and other matters. My front door was left a mess after they smashed it down, and they had the audacity to send me a bill for boarding it up after they smashed it.

I didn't pay that bill and never will, I should have made a claim against the police at the time, but I was dealing with far too much to take anything else on. I continued to work hard and started to clear my divorce settlement. The legal fees were mounting. I had no idea how I would survive. I had an outburst in court and called my wife's solicitor a bad name. My anger was not at my wife, but at her solicitors terrible provoking behaviour. I left a bad google review on the solicitor's firm's internet pages. I was then handed legal papers, as my wife's solicitor decided to sue me for hurt feelings. He was awarded over £6,700 damages and applied for over £16,000 legal costs. I had to pay it all and had no idea how as the interest was also being added to the debt. I wrote to her solicitor presenting him with an offer of settlement. It was a civilised letter, but he called the police, and I was arrested again. My legal adviser was very angry and was shouting at the police. I was taken back to the civil court and charged with a breach of orders, over £4,000 was added to his bill for stress caused. Apparently, the letter was harassing and breach an order to stay away from him, even though he written to me asking for me to attend his place of work and collect papers that very week. The matter was being handled dreadfully. I started to pay him thousands and began to struggle to pay my own bills. I even missed my mortgage payments at times because of it all. He once posted online attacks when responding to me, I was shocked at his behaviour. On a positive note, I was getting more and more work. I would continue to attend the family court regarding child access. I was asked by the judge if I feel I have done any wrong. I stated that day, 'I have not done any wrong and any married adult would respond to an affair with negative text messages and calls, you are daft to not think that wouldn't happen.' I also stated the same to Cafcass, who were ordered to carry out interviews and complete a report with recommendations.

I was instantly far from a fan of Cafcass, they should be abolished, I feel. Their report was completed but the Judge ruled it as being flawed and another report was ordered by the Judge. However, on the day of the interview for the second report to be completed. I received a call from a Cafcass officer who stated, 'We are unable to make the interview today, as we are understaffed, and we will just have to agree with the last report completed,' I couldn't believe my ears. The court stated that they have concerns that the text messages of harassment may continue, or I may bad mouth the mother to the children. It was recommended by the court that I complete a course that covered self-awareness. I disagreed with such recommendations at first and refused to start such a course, but seeing my children depended on it, so days after the hearing I contacted the court to agree in attending the course. I then find out because the course was only a recommendation. I would have to pay several thousand pounds, that I just didn't have spare. I had to beg the court over several months to turn the recommendation into an order, as this way there would be no charge. There was also a waiting list for the course, and it was eight months before I finally got accepted onto the course. Thirty men attended the first meeting, which was held at Bootle, Liverpool. I completed the six months' course, and I was the only one to have 100% attendance record out of over thirty men. I would have to walk many miles at times to get to the course, and most of the time cry all the way, as I missed my children, I couldn't handle being away from them. I am a good, loving, and caring father. I spent 14 months away from my children before getting them back. I came up with an idea of giving my eldest son two small silver bells. My eldest son would shake the bells at bedtime, saying to my youngest, that it was magic, and that it was dad saying goodnight. I had a separate set of bells that I would shake, and even began believing the magic myself, as I would shake the bells before sleep. My youngest son was still only very young, and I needed to create an idea that would make him think I was still with him. During the time I couldn't see my children. I would watch my eldest play football from a distance behind railings, and once whilst watching him. He spotted me and began crying in front of his teammates. I quickly left and started to walk home that day. However, my son peddled after me and cuddled me in the street. It became our secret seeing each other after football training. I admitted to the court during the final hearing, 2019, that I see him, and the Judge assured me nothing would happen by telling the truth. The judge at that final hearing stated, that I have never been a concern with harming my children. The judge also stated that day, that he refused to take the Cafcass report into account, which recommended just a few hours access per week. The Judge stated that it is of help to no one. He ordered that I have shared access again from that very weekend. He ordered that I have one overnight stay per week and after three weeks, it increases to two nights per week, building towards three nights per week. However, since that hearing, 2019. I have not been able to have any more than one night per week. The children's mother stated that the youngest had a routine that she didn't want to upset. My youngest was only around age six at this time and would have easily fallen into a new routine. I feel, sadly, that my youngest son now knows no different. It was all hard and I guess, there was never an easy solution with it all.

The day of the final hearing, I left court and cried with happiness. The relief was huge, and all I could do was cry. I sat at the Albert Dock, Liverpool and prayed. I often popped for Sunday service at the Liverpool Cathedral. I introduced myself to a reverend, he stated that he was concerned about me during the time I couldn't see my children. I was a mess when not able to see my children. It was a terrible experience that will live with me forever. I got my kids back, but it was hard. It was hard with my daughter, as she takes after me, and can be fiery. During the first few weeks of my separation, 2014. My daughter was shouting at me, she came at me aggressively, raising her hands at me. I struggled handling the situation, so I grabbed her, taking her to the front door, telling her to wait outside and that her mum will collect her. I would not have her shouting in front of my youngest, as he was just two years' old at the time of this incident. My daughter was collected that day from outside. I was upset for days after that evening, as I knew I could have handled it all better. I should not have shouted back, and simply ignored her. It was just hard, as I needed to protect my youngest son from the shouting. When I first shouted at her that day, she went upstairs calling me a bad name, swearing. I chased after her, banging on her bedroom door, saying how wrong she was and that I am calling her mum to collect her. On reflection I should never have banged on her door, as that was her private space. Being a parent is so hard at times, especially when being a single parent.

One evening whilst out walking I began praying in a park whilst alone. I asked God for help and guidance. I was asking him to guide me towards where I need to be. I told God I wanted to help people and become a better person, as I was sick of getting myself into situations. I do feel a victim of the system when not seeing my children and my legal adviser at the time agreed, but I still needed to improve as a man. I decided to study law, so I attended a local college for a short period. I then went onto study criminology, it was only for four months, just to get a taste for criminology, and to see if that was a route I wanted to take instead of straight law. I then attended a fast-track course at a university, before finally deciding and being entered on to a law degree, LLB. I completed a full-time three-year law degree and graduated with honours. I wasn't sure what to make of studying, it appeared a crazy idea at first, but studying allowed me to break away from my anxiety and struggle with PTSD. I began to feel strong mentally and I knew I was getting better in some small way. I struggled on the fast-track course at first, but it wasn't long before I picked up pace and began to find the course easy overall. I started my degree and would become friends with young students who were from all over the UK. I had it in my head that all students would be local, but this was far from the case. The first year was easy enough, the marks received would not count towards the final degree mark. The second-year things became a lot more difficult. It was harder for me, as I was still going through court, and those matters affected my studying. My marks were not great at the end of my second year. They could have been so much better; this is what annoys me looking back. I knew my final year I had to do much better, and thankfully, I did. I received a first in multiple subjects. I was lucky to be working with lovely tutors in my third year. My tutor for company law and tax were both lovely men, who have helped me with personal references since graduating. I finally completed university; it was a relief that It was over. All the hard work was worth it in the end.

The number of issues I had at times getting to university due to car troubles. It was almost impossible at times, but I still never missed a single lesson throughout the three years. My third year I was chosen to visit Strasbourg and Luxembourg to visit the European Court and the European Court of Human Rights, but sadly, Covid prevented students from travelling and I would miss out on the chance of a free holiday. I continued to study the last few months. I couldn't believe I was near the end of the degree. I was very nervous about what result I would be given. Results day was finally here, and I jumped for joy when seeing I achieved a high 2.1 grade. I finally felt that I had achieved something real. My graduation was booked, and I made my parents aware of the dates. They immediately complained, saying they had no idea how to get there. I arranged for a meal afterwards and stated I would pay for my own graduation meal and pay for everyone who attended. I asked my dad to at least pay for the graduation pictures, he refused and never bought them, despite that the cost was just £35.00. The day of the graduation involved me picking up my two sons. I had not seen my daughter for over two years at this stage. My daughter shouted at me over the phone, saying that she was upset that her mum lost at court and that I kept the main house, she also stated that her mum needed her name removed from the mortgage.

I was upset hearing this, as my daughter was young at the time, and didn't need to know what happened in court. My daughter didn't realise that the court experience cost me near £94,000 in total. I needed to try and not allow the fact that I had not seen my daughter affect me too much, as it was incredibly upsetting. If I allowed myself to get upset, it would affect me so much, it would even knock me off track with me achieving my goals. I needed to stay on track, as I was doing well with my studies and heading towards real achievements for once in my life. I wanted my daughter at my graduation so much. On the day when visiting the toilet, I got upset and cried that my daughter wasn't there. I made sure no one seen me upset, as to not cause embarrassment. My boys were dressed smart and seemed to enjoy the day. We had pictures taken and my parents were there too. My father refused to wear a suit, this annoyed me, but it was still nice to get some pictures of my parents next to me in my cap and gown. My boys appeared to be proud of me, I was hoping I was setting a good example. The day went well, and I received my reward, then left, heading to Lark Lane for an afternoon meal. My brother and his family attended, along with a close friend of mine, John. I didn't have much money and was disappointment my father didn't offer to pay for the meal, after all, he should have been proud of his son achieving a degree. The first degree achieved by anyone from his side of the family. My parents left early and rushed off home, and my brother left with them. I was left with my boys and a friend of mine. My friend offered to contribute towards the meal. I left happy that my boys got to see me achieve, that was all what mattered to me, but when getting home I was very upset thinking about my daughter. If only my daughter knew how hard I fought to winning back my children. If only she knew what I went through in getting my them all back. During the time I couldn't see my kids. I thought it was wrong that my wife turned up at my home with the kids and posted Father's Day cards, she was only doing what she thought was best for the children, I guess. I was unable to answer, or I would be in breach of court orders. I would have rather they didn't post them, as it was torture seeing them outside. The one incident that I feel affected my daughter more than any other was the time I received multiple calls from my daughter. This was during a time I was unable to talk to the children. I responded with two WhatsApp messages saying how much I loved her, and that I will send money to pay for any school trips or anything that she needs. I also added that she must be good for her mum and respect her as she works hard. My ex-wife called the police over that WhatsApp. A police officer came to me whilst I was working, but didn't arrest me, instead, allowing me to drive my van home. He came inside my home and stated, 'You are a good father and a good man, I have read the messages, and you have done no wrong in my eyes, but I am ordered to arrest you for breach of court orders.' He went onto say that I will not be handcuffed and not be treated like a criminal. The officer was a good man that day. I was not given bail and instead driven to Chester Crown Court where I was handed another two hundred unpaid hours and a suspended 18-month prison sentence. I should have pleaded not guilty again, as I was only responding to contact towards me. It would be very easy for me to blame my ex-wife for all. However, I can't blame her fully, as it was her solicitor who was the real person to blame, with his terrible advice and recommendations. My ex-wife was only following his advice and only doing what she thought was best, at the same time, I struggle to forgive her for allowing the applications to be put before the court, and other statements she made.

The family court experience, I feel, made matters worse for us all and it affected my children, certainly my daughter. The family court system almost encourages lies. Providing legal aid is one area, as if you use the word, abuse, you may be provided free legal aid. I will find it hard to forgive my ex-wife for some areas of the divorce process. Producing a statement which made out that I never took my children to school, when I took them and collected them daily, or stating, I let them down. I have never let my children down, other than one weekend when I failed to show as I went away for the weekend with a girlfriend. This was literally a one off over many years of always being there for my children and never letting them down. It was as though my ex-wife needed to make me out to be a bad guy to the court to get what she wanted, which a friend stated that it may be more of a divorce settlement, or the house. I just found the attacks in court strange, and I was confused by it all, but as stated. I do feel that most was driven by her legal adviser who was clearly causing issues that would create more legal fees. I would often pop back the doctors with stress. I was told that the divorce itself may have caused some PTSD, as not seeing my children affected me badly. It will live with me forever what I went through, it was wrong, My legal advisers voiced such on a regular basis. My legal adviser stated that I was the worst treated in any case he had handled, ever since starting out as a solicitor. I am a resilient person, as I always seem to get back up after being knocked down. When it came to my children, I would die fighting for them. I still get upset thinking how I struggled with money during the divorce. One stage during the divorce, my ex-wife took me to court at the advice of her solicitor for not paying the divorce settlement on time. I was a few thousand short and would be slightly late with the payment.

I was taken to court and awarded more time, but I was forced to pay my ex-wife's legal fees, of which were approximately £8,500. It was clear that my ex-wife's legal adviser was appearing to cause issues that would create more legal fees for him personally, without a care in the world how it affected the parties concerned. He was being very selfish during the whole process, even laughing at me on one occasion whilst in court. He stated to the Judge, 'Husband will only get £19,000 when we force sell the family home.' Thankfully I appealed and won that matter, the house was not forcibly sold, but I have not been able to get my ex-wife name removed from my mortgage due to the missed mortgage payments caused from pressure in paying him monies for his 'hurt feelings' matter. The charge on the home didn't help either that he has on it for his hurt feeling's debt, which is no benefit to his former client. There are some terrible legal advisers out there who appear to do whatever it takes to create extra legal fees, and without a care in the world for the children involved. I am aware so much of the bond I once had with my children has been destroyed by the divorce process. The family court creates so many issues at times, and as stated, especially the likes of Cafcass. What destroys the bond more so than anything else, is a parent who doesn't encourage the child to have a relationship with the other parent and who limits contact. This is unforgivable, sadly, this selfish and bitter behaviour is common today amongst separated parents.

Chapter Ten

Picking up the pieces

I went home after my graduation and my boys returned to their mums. I was left feeling lonely and sad. I reflected on my life that evening and sat up drinking wine until the early hours. I started to talk to a girl from Bournemouth and we got on well. I started to stay at Bournemouth at weekends. It wouldn't take that long to get there, certainly not as long as I first thought. I would leave at 8 a.m. and be there for 1 p.m. England is a lot smaller than people realise. The relationship got serious at speed, and she decided to move north and moved into my home. She had a young son the same age as my youngest. The relationship didn't last long because she had ex-boyfriends contacting her when they knew she was in a relationship. She refused to block them, and I had trust issues, which I guess were caused by finding out about an affair my ex-wife had, so I ended the relationship. I can't really say anything bad about the girl from Bournemouth, as she was a lovely girl. I just wasn't ready I guess, and it seemed right to end the relationship. She moved back to Bournemouth, and I have had no contact with her since. I wasn't really concerned about a relationship; I had no real want for one. I did become friends with a female locally, and we spoke daily, but it seemed unfair, as her daughter became attached to me, and I also started to feel attached to the daughter. She was an amazing and funny child. She would have me in hysterics laughing, as she would constantly wear spiderman costumes and other superhero consumes.

We once visited the cinema, and she wore a costume with a mask for the whole movie. If I ever had spare money, I would buy her a costume. We stopped talking and it may have been for the best, not that I didn't think a lot of this person, It was again down to trust issues. I didn't like the men she had been involved with, they seemed right idiots, and it appeared to me that she was still talking with then via social media. I am far from a social media fan; I find all the platforms terrible. You must take into consideration the child when one is getting involved. It is a whole package when getting with someone. You must think about how your presence can have an impact on the child. I totally disagree with children getting to meet multiple people. Thankfully, my ex-wife has only appeared to have had the one boyfriend, and I must be thankful for this as I would not want my children meeting different men. It was now time for me to pick up the pieces and try to rebuild my life. I sat and reflected often with how I had been a failure and disappointment. I would become angry, as I knew I was capable of so much more. I needed to create a plan of action, and I decided that I wanted to pursue a career as a barrister. I applied to complete my master's degree and the Bar Practice Course but would have to wait a year or two for my applications to be completed. It was now six years since I split with my ex-wife, and on a positive I had paid all my outstanding legal fees and divorce settlement. I only had the debt relating to the hurt feelings matter, which involved my ex-wife's legal advisor. This was causing me stress due to it being such a large sum. It was more annoying that it involved a very petty incident, which didn't cause any real harm if the truth was to be told. My daughter finished college, but I had no idea how she had got on, I was not even told what courses she had completed. My daughter applied to university, but I had no idea which university or what degree she would start. I was totally lost with why I was being treated in such a way. My eldest son struggled a bit at school, which made me worried, as I knew he wanted to do well and go to college, thankfully he managed to get onto a college course and at the college of his choosing. He appeared to be doing well, but I did receive a few calls from his tutor who was worried, as he was behind with his work. I was contacted by my eldest son out of the blue, who asked if the ground floor room could be turned into a 4th bedroom for him. I told him, yes, and instantly started to buy items in helping him to convert the room into a bedroom. I was extremely happy knowing he would live with me. My youngest son still stayed one day a week, even though I won shared access in 2019. I only ever got one day a week, I had been through far too much to go back court and fight for more time, so I had just accepted that I would only have one day a week. I get to watch my son at football and get to take him on holidays when I can. My children are happy and that is all what matters to me. I began praying a lot more and found comfort in doing such. I started to read more of the bible and thanked God daily for all I have, even though I have struggled a lot, I still have a lot to be thankful for. The last family holiday was around 2017. We had not been on a family holiday since and that breaks me, as my children deserve more. I have not been able to take my kids away either other than a few days out. My best memories I have are from my childhood are the ones on holiday with the family, and I wanted my children to have the same experience and memories. I got more work with the landscaping, but the work was drying up and we had long periods of many months without getting any work. My eldest son would always continue to help me with work, I would have been lost without him. Knowing my son was a room away brought me so much happiness. I was incredibly proud of him attending college and he appeared to be doing well, but the calls continued from his tutor who was concerned. I was again getting concerned and worried about my son as I thought that he may be struggling more than he was letting on, but he proved me and everyone wrong, as I received a call from his tutor who informed me that my son had achieved a distinction. I have never been so proud, I had tears of joy and just wanted to grab my son and scream from the rooftops. I was happy and proud of what he had achieved. My ex-wife called me concerned that my eldest son was considering not attending university. He had it in his head that he may want to do landscaping. My son called me asking me how many leaflets he would need to post to get work. I made it clear to him that it was all a risk, and the work was not steady. I made it clear that he must go on to university, I made him aware that he will have the time of his life. My son, thankfully agreed, and applied to attend university. He was accepted at Liverpool university to complete a business degree. My son would then move out and into rented student accommodation. I was upset to see him go, and I pleaded with him to come home for his second year to live with me, which would be rent free for him. I thought of how I could get out the house more, so I continued to play chess and would often visit Liverpool. This was a way of getting myself out and being around good people, as the people at the chess club were all decent. My old maths teacher from school who introduced me to a chess club, also attends the same club. It is nice bumping into him. He was probably the best teacher I have ever had, as he cared for students and went out of his way for me and my chess. I stayed friends with a few lads from the self-awareness course. They were decent lads, one or two just fell into the system like I did, when not really doing any wrong. The government has promised a complete shake up of the family court system, and it is needed, I feel, as it is a fine mess at times, causing more harm than good. This is the way I feel about it all. I just feel the figures speak for themselves, and there is good reason why the government has promised improvements. I would venture into Liverpool and meet with my mate from Anfield. We would pop to Liverpool one and sit outside, people watching. It was great getting back to Liverpool, as it brought back so many memories as a child when hanging around the city centre when bunking off from school. I still had no real vision of what I wanted to do as a career. I developed a love for studying and enjoyed it very much. I started to shadow barristers, which gave me the chance to complete mini pupillages. I decided that I wanted to pursue a career as a barrister for sure, especially after experiencing shadowing a few at court, but before I started that journey, I knew I needed to work on me. I knew I was a good man and knew that a lot of the situations I got myself in were not my fault. I was certainly treated badly when going through the divorce process. I was starting to feel much more mentally strong, and I was ready for change. I prayed daily and swore I would do whatever it took to set the best example before my children. I also wanted to help others as much as possible and give when I could. I felt I was a mess, a broken man, a man that needed to be rebuilt. I was a classic car that was battered and beat up, but under all that dirt and dust lay a classic that was priceless. I needed to believe in myself, and having children gives you motivation, or should do. I would only need to picture my kids to create energy. I still had lots of fight in me, and I reminded myself that I had a degree. I started to apply for more mini pupillages, and this gave me the chance to visit chambers and create contacts. If you wanted to apply for the Bar course in becoming a barrister, you needed a minimum of a 2:1 degree. You also needed to pass the basic entry tests, which included an advocacy assessment with a previous acting judge. You would be handed a case file. You needed to present a case before the judge via a zoom meeting. I passed all the entry requirements and entered on to the bar course with ease. I was finally on the road to a career that would make my family proud of me. I would call up my father daily with my progress, but he would constantly state that I would never become a barrister and from my perspective he seemed to enjoy pulling me down. I didn't care and even if I didn't make it as a barrister. I still didn't care, as I was now enjoying what I did. I wanted to study as much as possible and already had plans to complete two masters' degrees. I also wanted to complete my PHD one day. I started to find my passion in wanting to help and give as much as I could. I started an advert on social media stating I will award a single mum a free garden makeover. I chose a young girl and gave over six-hundred pounds worth of free materials and worked hard on the garden, but sadly they complained about the garden wanting more, which ruined the idea, but I didn't want that one experience to ruin my motivation. I would spend over £100 on flowers and drive around looking for woman to hand the flowers too. I gave flowers to a lollypop lady; it was amazing to see their smile when being handed the flowers. It was worth every penny to just see that smile. I also took my youngest son to the homeless shelter where we handed in old clothes, and on the way home my youngest turned to me and said, 'Dad I hope they like their new trainers.' My youngest had the ability to make me cry with love, due to the innocence he constantly spoke. He is such a lovely child, and he is growing into a fine young gentleman. I broke down when dropping him off at his mums one afternoon. He turned to me and said in his own words, 'Dad, wouldn't it be nice if we had a large table, we could all sit around it, and have dinner together.' In his little mind all he wanted was his family together. Divorce is a terrible thing when children are involved. I was having to deal with the struggles of PTSD caused by the experience at the family court, together with the upset caused in seeing how my children suffered being part of a divorce. I was still struggling with the PTSD from the shooting too. However, I was getting over that. I have been through so much in my life, and as stated, a lot of it was not caused by me, but most of it was. It was now time to pick up the pieces of destruction and rebuild myself as a man and as a father. I continued to visit the church at Liverpool for Sunday service when I could, and I took my boys along at times. I would tell them how I struggled when not seeing them for that terrible year. I don't think they will ever truly know what it was like for me not seeing them. I am sure they also struggled with it all as well. I have always been a good father, who cares and loves his children, and I have always provided. I now needed to get over it all and work hard in becoming the perfect man and father. I offered my ex-wife help and offered any form of support she needed. She would call occasionally for some help; she was very unwell during Covid and struggling, so I went around and helped. I grabbed an empty apple box and filled it with items to help her with the Covid. I bought, oranges, Lucozade, pain killers and many more items, along with a plant. I wanted my boys to see how a man should behave towards the mother of his kids. I did the same on my birthday, when out having a meal with my boys. I made sure that day, that the boys had flowers and chocolates for their mum when they returned home. I was still upset and struggling that my daughter didn't want to see me. She started to text me for money and items, such as trainers, ear buds for her mobile phone, and much more. I bought them all, but I never got a thank you and she didn't even come out to collect the items, instead sent my youngest out to collect the items I bought. I love my daughter, and it is my fault that I caused her to be upset with me. I started to nip away to hotels, treating myself to a B&B. I would travel to Essex and Wales. I bumped into a lad who I trained with, whilst boxing at Stoke. I went running with him and enjoyed that weekend catching up. It wasn't long before I bumped into other old mates who appeared upset that I distanced myself from them. I was getting invited to Bootle and other parts of Liverpool. I declined and made it clear I no longer go out to town centres, and they respected this and stated that they are there if I ever wanted a night out or if ever, I needed their help. One mate of mine was sentenced to six years in prison, I felt the urge to offer some help. I contacted his wife and asked if there was anything I could do to help. She asked only twice for help, and that was to drive the two daughters to Liverpool city centre when they needed to catch the train to London and the other help was collecting them all from the airport. I didn't hear anything from them after that, but years later the mate contacted me and thanked me for what I did. It was around 2019, and at this stage of my life my PTSD from the shooting was as good as gone. I had no issues with it at all, I was completely over it. I will always have a little shake once a while, I guess, or get paranoid when hearing a bang, but the moods, the up and down feelings were all gone. I still got upset when looking back at the year I didn't see my kids, this broke me completely and hurt me more than the shooting. I was suffering with not seeing my daughter, but my mind has trained itself to put it to one side, as I needed to protect my health. I started to read more and more, and I began writing too. I have good ideas for a play, I always wanted to write a play. The bar course start date was getting closer and closer. I was very excited about it all, but also nervous, as it would be the toughest course to date. The failure percentage rate was high, and this would cause some anxiety. I still had £9,000 outstanding with my ex-wife's solicitor, and he was trying to apply pressure in me paying it. He was trying to create more fees and add to the debt. The debt was clearly a source of income for him, and it is disgusting that it was ever in court. Work dried up with the landscaping and from 2021 I had as good as no work, so I needed to source other forms of work, so I started to apply for jobs. I was helping my dad when I could, and he would pass me some fuel money. I would literally get £20 for spending hours with him. Little did I know that my younger brother was being paid for working with my dad and good money. I was wondering why my dad was treating me so badly, as though I was not a son of his. He knew I had three children to support and provide for, as well as paying all the bills at my home myself. I felt like such a mug when finding out my dad paid my brother, and not me. It caused me even more upset when my brother had me driving him around for little bit of fuel money. I felt disrespected by my own family and treated like a fool. My brother wasn't to blame I guess, as he was only accepting the work. I feel my dad was to blame for the treatment towards me. I also blame my dad for a breakup between my brother and sister. I found out that my sister was ignored by my dad when she needed a place to stay for her and her youngest daughter. It breaks my heart knowing that at that time I lived alone in my own house, and I would have allowed them to stay and use the house as their own. Thankfully, a year or so later my sister met an amazing man and today they are happily married. I would literally do anything for my sister, and brother-in-law, especially anything for their kids. I love them all. My dad would get a kick out of sickening things at times. Me, my brother, and sister arguing, was only the tip of the iceberg. My dad once bought a pellet gun to shoot hawks that would chase his pigeons. He once pointed it at my face in the garden to see my reaction, as he knew I suffered with PTSD. It was vile looking back, as I could feel myself shaking inside with fear as the gun was pointed at me.

Chapter Eleven

The road to the Bar

It was 2022 and it was the year that I would start the bar course. In the run up to my first day, I would contact my father daily and inform him with how I was progressing with it all. He seemed impressed and proud of what I was achieving. I attended the induction day at the university and the other students all appeared excited and up for the challenge. I have developed an ability for weighing people up at speed, these are skills that I gained whilst I held the role of a Regional Manager during my time working in Irish transport. I could see that a few of the students possessed a terrible attitude. It was scary to think that some of them would one day become barristers. The madness of the diversity tick box made it easier, I feel, for many who are not suited to a career at the bar, being offered pupillages. Family law appears addicted of late to only taking on females. I spoke with a head of HR at a large Liverpool law firm who stated that most chambers who specialise in family law will only take on females these days. She also stated that roles, such as a paralegal in family law that I have applied for I may struggle with, due to being male, and she was correct, as I was not successful for any of those roles despite having more than enough experience and academic ability. The induction day had very limited information, not all was made clear on the day, such as if you fail the bar course but pass the master's degree. The course does not allow you to take the master's degree that you may have passed with you.

I feel there was good reason why this was not highlighted on the induction day. It was almost a con, resembling what you may find on a Vegas gambling strip. They provide limited information to tempt you in, but once in, not all is what it first appears to be, but it's too late now to do anything as they have your money. I found a few tutors difficult to speak to, it was as though it was painful for them to speak with you, as for some reason, they thought that they were above you in some way. My personal tutor was a good example, a complete snob with a vile attitude. I was far from impressed with a few of them, but at the same time, there were amazing and genuine people, such as a female criminal tutor, who was just lovely. We were handed the criminal procedures book, along with the civil procedures book. These were very heavy and expensive books that were needed for such a course. The value of the books combined was over £2,000. I got home and began reading. The books made me very anxious about the whole course, as they were difficult to understand. Every day I pictured myself wearing a barrister's wig in a court room, whilst representing a client. The image made me feel proud, it made me feel that I was becoming a better person, but I would argue with myself at times. I would remind myself that I do not need to become a barrister in order, to be accepted by society. There are many other options that I could pursue with becoming more successful and setting a good example for my children. I just became obsessed with the idea of becoming a barrister, but when I think long and hard about it all. I don't think the role would be for me. I had been told so many times when growing up that I was a failure and a bad person who was going nowhere in life. I was looked down on so many times when attending court for minor offences as a youngster that it developed an attitude towards the legal profession.

I guess I wanted to prove to them that I was just as good as them, and becoming a barrister was a good way of me proving such. My divorce was the biggest test of my life, being away from my children tested me to my limits. I am a very resilient man; the best ability I possess is always being able to bounce back after being knocked down. There is something inside me that refuses to give up. It is extremely powerful, as it has a great deal of patience. It can wait and accept that certain things take much time. These are all great qualities, but only if used correctly. I would constantly picture my ex-wife's barrister who was an absolute idiot. The pathetic joke of a man who refused to go into a private room with me, and instead discussed my private family matters in a public waiting room, of which goes against the rules, and procedures. The same joke of a man who brought up a historic driving offence that was over twenty-five years ago during a child arrangements application. How is all that relevant or in the child's best interest at all. We wonder why the family court is a mess at times. I would also picture the Judges who worked on my family matter, and how they were absolutely sickening, especially the first two judges who handled matters. They were clueless with what was in the best interest of the child. These experiences would race around my mind regularly and motivate me in achieving my goal of being called to the bar. It was as though I developed a personal vendetta against the legal system. The system that is a mess, and is, I feel, causing more harm than good in a lot of cases. They destroyed my children, and I have not seen my daughter in six years because of the family court and the damage it and Cafcass created. I had so much anger in me, and the only way I could release it all was to become a barrister. I distanced myself from the students, as stated, a good few had awful attitudes. I was entered into the WhatsApp group, but I removed myself after a couple of weeks.

I am so glad I had the influence of my grandparents growing up, it is something that is lacking today. I always use 'please' and 'thank you'. I speak with anyone and would help anyone too. I never judge or treat people differently. However, I also treat people how they treat me. I speak to people nice at first, but if I come across a snobbish or rude personality, they are gifted with a different approach. The course was draining and very demanding, as there was so much to it. I managed the master's degree without issue and enjoyed such, but the bar course was something I struggled with in areas. I had no issue in applying the law and linking needed issues. It was the written side of matters, the structure of papers that I struggled with at times.

The young trouble kid was popping back in me from time to time. The want to cause issues or argue an irrelevant point. My childhood certainly affected me well into my adulthood. It was scary how much the abuse could still have an impact. My mother continued the abuse well into my adulthood. Her constant swearing and shouting at me for no reason. I would often get, 'what the fuck do you want?' when I simply turned up to their home to make my dad aware how I was getting on. When I was not about, my mum would attack someone else. I firmly believe that my father's high blood pressure was caused by the stress of my mum over the years. I still remember seeing my dad cry with frustration due to my mum's behaviour. My father was bullied and abused by my mum countless times I believe. I was becoming excited at the thought of being barrister, but when I examined my feelings, it wasn't so much the role that excited me, but the status that came with it all. One thing I developed over the past ten years up to this point, was a good level of self-awareness. I was very aware of my issues and would try to address them as much as I could.

I was aware that one should only want to become a barrister for the right reasons. They want to seek justice, to gain the best and fair outcome for all parties, especially if it's a family matter. I did possess a passion for family law and child protection, sadly, I lost this due to an experience I had whilst attending a mini pupillage. I sat in a room listening to barristers and social services discuss a matter. They laughed on a few occasions, stating that it was no wonder that the kids are messed up due to how their case was being handled by all departments. I didn't find it amusing and certainly didn't laugh. In fact, I shed a few tears on my way home that day when thinking about how those children must be suffering in the hands of these terrible people. This is the issue with today, no one has a passion to be better, or to do better. They just collect a pay cheque and go home to a glass of wine. I would take my work home emotionally, I just know it would all get the better of me, as I would want to do better and become frustrated when departments let down the children I represented. This is why I started to think about different career ideas. I completed a child mentor course in Manchester, of which I enjoyed. This was a chance to help children who had become victims of bad parenting, or who simply suffered mental illnesses that caused behaviour problems. It was a chance to carry out a hands-on roll. I thought it would be so much more rewarding, yes, I am aware much less pay, but so what, life isn't about money. The day you think life revolves around money is the day you fail at life. I feel life should be about finding a passion and the love of doing such. I always wanted to help others, and often look for voluntary work. The child mentor course was a voluntary course that had the promise of a role at a school once you completed all needed criteria. This was the first encounter I had with the dreaded DBS check. I have three convictions on my DBS. I have a conviction for asking my ex-wife what the papers were that were thrown at my face, no violence took place when asking her what the papers were. It was a question put across in a peaceful and civilised manner. My biggest regret I have is pleading guilty to that matter, instead of correctly pleading not guilty to the breach of the order. The second conviction is a caution for calling my ex-wife's lover when asking when the affair started, and the third conviction was the two WhatsApp messages I sent in response to my daughter who was asking for money. I am a perfect example how the family court can criminalise a loving parent. I was refused a role of child mentor with the Manchester company due to these three convictions I had on my file. I had no restriction in working with adults or children and never have done. The issue with schools and companies like the child mentor firm, is that they don't understand the matters they view on a DBS. They just see convictions and it scares them. It caused me much frustration, as so many teachers these days are wrong for the role, and yet, here is me, a decent man who could offer so much and who would be an ideal candidate for a child mentor role, as I can relate to children who misbehave. It felt like, oh here we go again, hurdles and obstacles placed before me, victimised yet again. Society has it all so very wrong, and this is why we have so many issues. This is why we have so many young students being offered pupillages who have nothing other than a terrible attitude, the diversity tick box has so much to answer for. The three convictions on my DBS all relate to a civil matter. The civil burden of proof is much lesser than that of criminal. The civil burden of proof is the balance of probability. I have no convictions on my file other than a driving offence when age seventeen. I enter the family court system, and I become a criminal, for merely asking what the papers were, or replying to my daughter to make her aware I will transfer her money. Yes, one could state that it is a breach of court orders, and yes, it is, but common sense should prevail. Courts should look at all the facts and read the WhatsApp, if it's of no harm, as it was in my case then a warning should take place and nothing other. I started to dislike the family court system the more I got to know it. I firmly believe that if my ex-wife knew what was involved and if she knew what would have happened, she never would have started the process. I was very alone in my life during the bar course, I guess I was very alone in my life since 2016. I got used to being alone and I would often block out the upset I had inside, such as missing my daughter. If I started to think about the fact my daughter didn't see me, it would make me cry uncontrollably for many hours. I started to apply for more mini pupillages and more shadowing of Judges. The shadowing of a circuit Judge at Manchester was an amazing experience. She was the loveliest person you could wish to meet. However, at the same time I would not like to be before her if committing a crime. I started to gain more passion for criminal law, oppose to family law. I know that this is down to the fact that the family court is a bit of a mess and in need of complete reform. I am aware criminal have their own issues, but for me, nowhere near as much as the family court. I would often pop to the library, and I would sit alone, daydreaming for hours. When I read family related case law it would often bring back my awful experience, which I feel has caused some PTSD. I have noticed that when I talk about the experience at the family court, I start to feel tense and get upset, just as I do when talking about the shooting incident. There was so much to the bar course, you had to join an inn of court at London, which was a difficult choice at first. When applying to join an inn of court, it included a vetting process, which meant having to declare any convictions one may have. I didn't realise this was part of the process, and only realised when a few months into the bar course. I declared my convictions, which meant I would then be involved in having to attend an interview with a panel of three judges, and this was an extremely scary process. They had all my details and went through each conviction in much detail. The interview started off with a female judge saying, 'so, you don't think judges know what they are doing?' I replied with a shake in my voice, 'I am sorry?' The judge looked down her glasses and went on to say, 'You appealed a few decisions in your family matter, which indicate that you disagreed with the judge's decision, which is why I stated that you appear to think that judges do not know what they are doing.' I was not prepared for these types of questions at all, I didn't really know what I was in for, but never expected that. I replied, 'I won two appeals at the Higher court when representing myself, so the Higher court certainly agreed with me not agreeing with the lower decisions.' The judge quickly flicked through the documents saying, 'Oh, yes, I see.' I appeared to win round one of what seemed to be a battle. There were many more difficult questions in the near two-hour interview. I coped well and at the end of the interview I was told to wait. They had me waiting for nearly one hour before making me aware that they had decided that I am proper enough to become a barrister. I was overjoyed but didn't really understand why. I guess it was hearing the words of acceptance again that made me feel more part of society. I am aware that my childhood affected me as an adult. The constant rejection at schools, or the constant abuse at home. The words of my mother that would constantly hit me like a brick to the chest. The verbal attacks I suffered almost daily by my mum would affect me for the rest of my life. To be swore at daily and suffer a weekly beating, which at times involved the butt of a pool cue would damage me in so many ways. What upset me most was that to the outside world my mum was the nicest person alive. My girlfriends loved her, but they didn't see what I had witnessed behind closed doors. I was being treated like a puppet on a string, as my mum would show me love a lot of the time, which confused me and played with my emotions even more so. Once my lessons finished, I would always rush back to my car at the Mount Pleasant car park. I would feel excitement on my journey down the long road towards the car park. Once I got to my car, it suddenly hit me that I had nothing to get home to. My children didn't live with me, and I had no one at home to greet me. I would always start to feel slightly upset, so I would drive to my mums on the way home and tell my dad how my day went. He would be laying on the sofa in the front side room looking tired at times. My parents have a beautiful house. There are two living areas at the front of house and a side extension.

There is a well in the kitchen area where the servants once washed clothes, as the rear of the property must have at one point been the servants' quarters. My mum would often sit by the other living area, usually drinking wine. It was clear that she had a drink issue, as she had two personalities. The one who hadn't drank was never a nice person towards me, but once having a few glasses of wine she would perk up and suddenly show me love. It was horrible having the love you yearned for from a parent, but then, in a blink of an eye, the love would disappear, and a verbal attack would start. My love was constantly up and down with my mum, and this certainly affected me as a person. I would go home after visiting my parents and read as much as I could. I understood law well and I knew how to apply it, but I was still struggling with the structure of my work, and this is what would have an impact on my grades. The master's side of the course was going well. I chose family law as my master's subject, and this was an area I knew well. I sailed through my master's degree and ended up getting a high merit grade. I would sit in the park near the university once the day had finished. I would sit and picture watching my children play, I miss them being young. Not seeing my daughter was affecting me more than I realised. I would go for a meal alone after university at times and imagine that my daughter was sitting across the table from me. I would imagine we talked about how she was getting on, and even imagine us laughing and joking about. I became numb to upset, it was as though I had no more tears left inside me at times. My body dried up of tears, I would instead just sit and stare at the ground. The bar course had its issues, and I guess that is because I don't take too kindly to snobs. That's the best way I can put it, many barristers have a terrible snobbish attitude, and I have no idea why, as there is nothing special about them at all. I had to complete 10 to 15 qualifying sessions as part of the course. The qualifying sessions would be run by the inn of court at London. This involved attending London for discussions about diversity, pupillage applications, advocacy, and some areas of law. I attended a diversity session, and a young female of colour would speak, she was a barrister. She was the perfect example of a terrible attitude. She spoke about how colour is the only issue relating to diversity, she also highlighted how disgusted she was when a court member of staff simply asked her if she was a witness. She stated that it was racist to not immediately think that she was a barrister. I highlight that she was about twenty-four years of age, I feel anyone could have made that mistake. My point is this attitude is tolerated at the bar and almost encouraged. I spoke out stating, 'If you think colour is the only issue at the bar, you would be very naïve, as an example, people with northern accents have just as many issues at the bar as other diversity issues.' The young female barrister had completed her little speech at this point, but decided to come back at me, which I was not allowed to respond too. I feel there are many diversity issues in society today, the moment a London barrister hears a scouse accent, as an example, you can see that they look uncomfortable. It was time for my residential weekend, and I chose Windsor. I wanted to go south for my residential stay. This stay involved many qualifying sessions during the weekend. Approximately fifteen Judges would be present and twenty barristers. Students would be separated into teams of three and allocated a Judge and barrister who would prepare students for the day's exercises. I remember the first day of the weekend residential stay, a member of staff of the inn of court didn't like me, and this was because during a previous dinner and tie evening I went for a drink with a female student who approached me. We discussed the bar course and that was it, but this staff member didn't like this for some reason. The member of staff's attitude was terrible to say the least. She was almost aggressive towards me during the weekend, I simply ignored her as much as I could. At the end of the first introduction to the weekend, we went into a room for drinks and a chance to socialise. I walked up to two senior older barristers, one was a KC. I said hello, I was polite with my approach. However, the older male when hearing my slight Liverpool accent looked down at me and walked away. I am far too experienced to have misjudged this situation. I had wined and dined directors of many blue-chip companies and ran near two hundred staff. I can weigh up a situation at speed. This person was just a snob, and that is the best way of putting it. A young male student approached me in a very direct manner asking with a posh tone, 'where are you from?' I replied, 'I am originally from Liverpool, but have lived in Cheshire the past twenty-five years.' To my absolute shock, he responded with, 'oh deary me' and walked away. One hour passed and I was starting to feel out of place, not because these were well to do people, as I have mixed with many millionaires before today when wining and dining directors during my career in transport. Including directors of B&Q, Astra Zeneca, and many more. I was feeling out of place as I am a decent, nice lad, and many of these people were rude. I do highlight that 80% were lovely people and the supervising barrister who was a KC that I was allocated, was brilliant, such a lovely guy. A lot of the students were nice too, but there were a small percentage who were just rude, I feel. I am shocked at this, because if I wanted someone to represent me, I wouldn't want some snob, I would want a nice person who would get the jury, as an example, on their side. Overall, the residential weekend was an amazing experience, as It was the Royal Family's estate. I had the chance to walk around and visit all areas of the estate, including the workshops where young apprentices were given the chance to learn a trade. King Charles created the idea, I believe. The staff on the estate were lovely, and very approachable. During the last two days I met a group of five students. They were lovely people, and I have added them onto social media and kept in touch. I drove to Windsor in my old Land Rover Freelander, and embarrassingly, it would not start on the last day, and I needed a jump-start from a groundsman. I also took a wrong turn and ended up on the Royal family's horse-riding track. I finally made it out of the estate and made my way home, but during my way home I would feel slightly upset with the fact that I couldn't tell my grandparents about this stay, as they would have loved to have known about the estate at Windsor. I returned home and would immediately drive to my dad, telling him all about my experience. At times when I was speaking to my dad, my mum would frown in the background, as though she was jealous. I remember as a young child, I was playing with a fishing rod, and the hook became caught in my hand. I cried in pain, and my father came rushing to help me.

He got the hook out of my hand and cuddled me, but as I looked over his shoulder, my mum was laughing, saying, 'ah dad, I love you.' She was clearly upset or annoyed that I didn't run to her, but why would I? She was always aggressive, always shouting and swearing. I continued the bar course, but would have many issues, as train strikes prevented face to face learning. We would be forced to have remote lessons; this was not what I paid for. I didn't learn as well when the lesson was remote. I was annoyed to learn that during another train strike, I would be forced to still make my way into complete my assessment. This was simply down to the fact that it was almost the last day, and the tutors were attending a leaving event, so it suited them to then have face to face. I struggled, as there were bus issues that day. I had to walk six miles in the heat whilst wearing a suit. I then got the bus from Whiston to Liverpool and walked from the bus station to the university.

By the time I got to the university I was dripping with sweat and very tired, certainly not prepared for an advocacy assessment. It was wrong, but universities appear to do whatever suits them. I am far from a fan of universities; they are a business and the support they offer is also lacking from what I experienced. The most difficult assessments with the bar course are the Civil and Criminal litigation. These would be completed remotely. I agreed, as I assumed that the software that would be used would be suitable and contain no issues. However, it was not, and I suffered many tech issues. The screen would close if your face moved out of shot, but the questions were at the bottom of the page and you had to bend down to read them, especially is wearing glasses, as I do, due to these issues I failed all my remote assessments. I feel that some results were biased, as I made it clear that I didn't like my personal tutor, and I have a little sneaky feeling that her husband who is also a barrister may have at some point been involved in my private matters, It was just a few little things I picked up on. I would have to start arranging resits, even though I complained about the fact I had tech issues, but the complaints were ignored, so many had the same issue, but the university, as stated, just appear to do whatever suits them. I started to pass my resits, I had twelve to complete to be called to the bar and pursue a pupillage in becoming a barrister. I passed all my advocacy assessments and my opinion writing, which was a very tough assessment. I was shocked that my remote drafting assessment was failed, What shocked me was the feedback I received, as the feedback didn't seem to match my paper submitted. It was marked down for a spelling error, which was ridiculous, since this was limited timed assessment, but I was marked down as it stated I wrote my own name, which I know for a fact I didn't. I wrote the anonymous name of Mr A Barrister. I immediately requested a copy of the paper I submitted via the online remote assessment page, so I could match the feedback, and the paper submitted. It was refused, why would anyone refuse to provide a copy of a submitted paper. It was starting to feel corrupt, and even more so when I discussed my issues with many other students. Yet again, here I am in life having issues; why can't I just have a smooth sail? The one thing that was upsetting me was the fact that they would take away my master's degree that I had passed if I fail the bar course. I was still very upset during this time, but I still applied for a pupillage when the pupillage window opened. I guess I applied to again to prove a point. It is extremely difficulty to gain a pupillage, especially if you are a white male, or so it seems. I was offered two interviews, and this alone was an amazing achievement. The facts are, if I can walk in a win a £5 million contract that contained around £1.4 million pure profit, and if I can walk into the Higher courts and win my appeal whilst a litigant in person, then surely, I can walk into a pupillage interview and win a pupillage. I decided to not attend the pupillage interviews, because if I got them but failed the bar course it would have been too much for me to handle. I would not allow failing areas get to me too much, as I had this ability to keep pushing forwards. In the run up to my bar assessments, I already started preparing for failure, I applied to carry out a second master's degree in Sunderland. My aim was to complete my PHD. This would leave a mark on the family history and make my children extremely proud. I would be able to sign as a doctor, which would always provide me with a sense of achievement and acceptance. I continued to try my best with the bar course and would revise as much as I could. Living alone was one bonus when studying, as no one was there to disturb me. It would have been nice to be in a relationship at times, because it would've been nice to discuss case law with someone else. I had got so use to getting home to an empty house, grabbing a bowl of seeds for the birds, then throwing the bowl in the garden.

I would then sit and wait for the birds to pop along; this was the only enjoyment I seemed to have at this stage of my life. I would often look back over my life and wonder why I misbehaved at school, why I wasted so much time, and why I ruined a couple of decent relationships. I would look back at my experience in the army, visualising myself as a young lad, wanting to go back in time and give myself a good talking to. I still often look at a few of the bar students on social media. The ones I added on social media were all part of the nice bunch. I look at them all gaining pupillage and feel low about myself, as I feel I am so very far behind them.

I feel that I should be with them and part of the group, but I have been struggling with it all the past year. I must stay focused and not beat myself up so much, I remind myself of this as much as possible.

Chapter Twelve

My Dad

I continued with the bar course and popped into the university library when I could, as we were in our last few weeks, and I needed to revise as much as possible. I still had eight assessment resists outstanding, and these last two weeks would be my last chance to gain advice from other students and tutors. It was the day of a civil advocacy lesson. I sat there daydreaming, starting to feel sad for some reason and had no idea why. The next minute the university receptionist came into the class asking for me. I went to a private room where she told me that my dad had been rushed into hospital. I called my brother's partner who was kind enough to come and collect me from university and drive me to the hospital; The previous evening my father had a huge headache, my mother called for an ambulance, but was told it may be five hours wait. She drove my father to the hospital where they were forced to wait in the A&E department. This makes me angry, as my father had stroke symptoms. He was left in the corridor for hours, and finally told he had a brain tumour that was very serious as the bleed was large. I never would have allowed my father to go to Warrington hospital. I hate the place and would have drove him to Liverpool. I am still upset and angry that my mother didn't call me to help. Even on the night of the incident, she had her sister there and not me or my sister. When seeing my father for the first time in the bed, he had many tubes around him and was connected to a life support machine. It hit me hard, and I suffered shock.

It didn't seem real, and I struggled to digest the situation. My father lasted just a few days before they decided to switch off the life support machine. I was angry and wanted answers why my father was left in the corridor. Even whilst in hospital my mother was terrible towards me, and even my eldest son. In an aggressive manner, she shouted out the blue for my eldest son to leave. It makes me angry thinking about how she has abused me and caused so much upset to us all over the years. My mum, brother and sister walked to the café, I stayed with my dad and prayed for the Lord to accept him into heaven, it was important to me to complete these prayers. My mum suddenly turned up, frowning, and asking me what I was doing.

I completely ignored her, I wasn't going to take any more abuse from her, certainly not at that moment. I videoed my father just two days before he went into hospital. He was in good spirits, and I get upset that I didn't walk to the shop with them that evening. My mother shouted at me that evening, attacking me saying, 'you never get us anything, you never do anything.' She clearly forgotten all the flowers I would take her. The heavy steel royal mail post box that cost me hundreds during a time that I had no money. The £300 handmade jewellery box, the many pictures in her house. Only a month before this verbal attack I purchased a £320 small French cabinet from an auction. I had just £550 in the bank at the time when purchasing this item. I would always do my best to win her affection, and I have no idea why. I guess when you are abused from a young age, the abuser always seems to have a hold on you. You are like a trapped fish on a hook. I watch the last video of my dad repeatedly, and it still doesn't seem real that he is gone. He worked so hard, buying his first store very young and retiring at a young age. His plan to emigrate to Portugal was all planned and as good as arranged, this is why the recent holiday to Portugal with my cousin meant a lot, as I got to see what my dad wanted from life. My dad was always slightly overweight and never seemed to exercise much. This is why I have been so health conscious in my life and always kept my fitness at a good level. The experiences at the hospital the few days that my father was alive was a strange one. My sister was very upset, along with me, but outside my brother appeared in good spirits, laughing at one point whilst smoking a cigarette with my mum. The pair of them were sitting with each other, talking in private, but then stopping when I approached. It was as though a new family was formed and me and my sister were not part of it. When my sister was young, she was the most beautiful child you could ever see, she was so funny too. My sister would sit for hours playing with her Barbie dolls, sit chatting away to herself. If she were my daughter, I would be nothing but extremely proud. She is a perfect mother, with a lovely family. Her husband is probably the nicest man I have ever met. It makes me very upset to think I once bad mouthed the pair of them with my brother and parents, but as stated, this was part of growing up in our household. You would get dragged in to slagging others off and disliking people, when not really thinking why you dislike them. My parents had a strong influence on all of us growing up. On the day after my father's passing, I was to complete a civil advocacy session. I felt pressured into speaking in front of many students while putting forward a civil matter, whilst the tutor played the role of the judge. I was being recorded at the time, but halfway through I broke down in tears. I felt embarrassed as many students watched me. I left the building and walked towards the car park at a slow pace. Not once did the university call me that day to see if I got home okay.

I didn't feel that my father had gone and kept thinking I could call him. I was disgusted to learn that my brother had my father's mobile phone and would read messages that were sent, even messages that me and my sister sent. I was also upset to learn that my brother started work on transferring the pigeon business into his own name, appearing to protect his share, which he seemed to now be trying to increase. Me and my sister were completely unaware of the goings on that my brother was up to. We visited my mother, she was very upset crying and saying that a thousand pounds was missing from my father's wallet, days later my mum stated that my brother needed the money for fuel. My sister became angry, my sister probably never knew this, but I would always protect my sister, even during a time we didn't speak. I have always loved her very much, even during a time I bad mouthed her with my brother and parents. I didn't say anything very bad, I just joined in, as I foolishly believed the lies that my brother and parents was saying about my sister and her partner. They had an ability to have you join in and agree with them. Thankfully, the last few years I distanced myself from joining in and instead I would be quiet. I even sent Christmas cards to my sister, as I knew bad mouthing anyone was wrong, especially when there was nothing to bad mouth about. My sister has fire, and we are alike in many ways. She will probably disagree with that, but she would be wrong, as we are alike. My sister became angry and rightly so, she was only protecting my fathers' interests and my mothers. My sister had a huge argument and left, but the day after I returned to my parents where my brother was sat at the sofa with his partner, my mother was in the kitchen area. My brother started to talk about money, but I noticed my mother signalling to my brother to stay quiet and to tell me nothing. As I studied law for many years at this point, I knew that they had an obligation to make me and my sister aware of the estate value, but me and my sister simply wanted no part and instead walked away. I haven't seen my mum or brother from that point, which is extremely sad. Today my brother has fitted a doorbell to my parents' home and watches who visits. There are also cameras inside the home, which I find concerning, as it appears that he is controlling my mum, I feel. My mum has not once sent me or my sister or our children any birthday cards or Christmas cards since my father's passing, and that is now near two years at this point. My sister and her husband paid for all the food at the funeral, they didn't need to do this, as my mum had money from my father's account. My brother also had access to the account too, but they allowed my sister, and her husband pay for the funeral food, which was a lot. They never even got a thank you, even on the day they were ignored. I was embarrassed and annoyed at this. My brother-in-law should never have paid anything, but he is that decent he just went ahead with it. He is also that nice that he wasn't bothered he didn't get a 'thank you' and was ignored. He is simply better than it all, and I admire him for that. Me and my sister begged for items of my fathers to remember him by, as we were struggling with the loss. I had been receiving medication and counselling in dealing with the loss and having a few of his items would have helped in a small way, but my mother refused to give us any items, until one day we got the news that a few bags of items had been passed to our auntie to give to us. I was very disgusted when learning that the items handed to us were only a few suits that he never wore, but within the bags were pictures of our children and of us as children. There was also a large, framed logo that my daughter drew as a young child, a logo that won a competition in being picked as a new school logo and would be shown on all uniforms from that point. This logo made my father so very proud and for my mum to return it, was very disturbing behaviour.

This was a perfect example with how nasty my mum could get and for no reason at all, as me and my sister had not been anywhere near my parent's home for over a year at this point. I would cry several evenings every week since my father passed, I struggled badly with it. I was contacted by my inn of court to apply for a scholarship in April 2023, which would involve many months of checks, including interviews. It was decided after several months by a panel, that I would be awarded a scholarship. This involved being handed a cheque for funds to pay towards my student fees.

I walked outside on to the grounds of the inn of court, and I looked to the sky with excitement. I knew that this award would assist my CV in being chosen for a pupillage if making it that far. I grabbed my phone and typed in the first six digits of my father's number to tell him the news, before releasing that my father had been gone seven months at this point. I immediately began to cry, as it was another harsh reminder that he had gone. I walked until I found a quiet bench and sat for hours speaking to my dad and making him aware of my achievements. Although I was always very much alone since my divorce, I still had good people around me. A good friend at the chess club I represent who is a neurologist, he has provided me with several references. This person is just the nicest person you could wish to meet, and I don't say that because he has helped me. Ironically, I was contacted by this person who asked if my father had passed. He was aware of my father's details and made me aware that nothing could have been done, and in a small way this helped me, as I trusted my friend's word. I needed to find work as I was struggling with money. It was hard living alone and having to pay all the bills by myself. I was aware I was not well enough to work, but I had no support and no one to turn to.

I would go without food for days, and tell myself it was a good thing, as there are benefits with fasting. I managed to find a job at a local call centre which was only two train stops from my local train station. It went okay for the first few months, and I started to enjoy speaking to the customers who called in, but at times I would struggle. I would have to pop to the toilet when getting upset about my dad. I would hide my tears, and always put on a brave face that all was ok at. I informed my supervisor that I was struggling, but no adjustments were ever made for me.

I was moved to a different team and gained the courage to hand over a letter from my GP which detailed how I was struggling with my depression due to the loss of my father, but the manager didn't seem to care and again turned a blind eye to the fact I struggled at times. I eventually had a bad experience at this workplace and was forced off work sick. The manager shouted at me and treated me awfully. I started an employment tribunal claim, as I was not going to allow anyone to treat me badly. This was not about gaining money from a claim, this was about me standing my ground for what was right. I continued my weekly counselling sessions, but I still very much struggled. I found comfort in speaking to my dad when I was alone and telling him my plans. I could almost hear his words of advice for me to get my act together and fight for a life. It was 2024 and I was still very much single and had been single since November 2021. There was only one person who I had met a few times and that was the person who I needed to cut off, out of respect for her lovely daughter and for her too, as I knew it couldn't go anywhere due to her male friends that I was aware she was still in contact with, who I didn't like at all, and for good reason. I began to get addicted to my own space and being alone, I even distanced myself from the few good friends I had at this time. I have many friends who I have known over the years throughout the UK and Ireland, but I distanced myself from them all. I have always enjoyed my own company, ever since the days of playing snooker on my own in the garage whilst we lived at Gentwood Road, Huyton. I started to walk the route my father walked and would almost feel that he was with me. I also drove to Huyton and walked around Bruton Road, and Gentwood Road. I would imagine my grandparents were still alive and my father. I would pretend we had full blown conversations, even imagining my grandmother saying how proud she was of me. This helped me a lot, as I would always imagine them telling me to fight and keep pushing forward. I was off work for several months before looking how I could follow any passions I had. I always enjoyed helping kids, I would complete another child mentor course, which would allow me to add to my CV. I completed several online courses which covered safeguarding in schools, but sadly I struggled still in gaining a post due to the ridiculous small minor civil convictions on my DBS. The schools would notice these matters and without even asking what they were, they would refuse me, of which is or may have been discrimination. I finally handed my notice in for constructive dismissal, I was forced to due to the working environment being an intimidating one. It would be unreasonable for me to return to such an environment. This allowed me the time to start writing, which helped me in so many ways. It was as though at first, as I was releasing so much weight from my shoulders. As I wrote the many words onto paper, the troubles became less of a weight hanging over me. I began reading the bible more too, this brought me comfort. I would pray for my parents and ask that my mother be forgiven for how she has been and how she is. I would ask God to help her, and to also forgive my brother. I have always believed that good things happen to good people and bad things always seem to happen to bad people. My grandmother would say similar words to that of my father when it came to life advice, *'you end up with what and who you deserve in life, from how you have lived life and who you are.'* This is very true; these words would repeat in mind my constantly. I have so many memories with my father, especially when it was just him and me, as it was clear I was far from my mother's favourite. I can still remember almost every moment of the evening I spent the night with my father whilst he was a security guard at the fruit market on Edge Lane, Liverpool. We sat in a little hut, and I listened to my father telling me stories about the different people who would visit the market. One afternoon an old man got out of what appeared to be a very old little van. My dad asked me if I thought he was rich, I replied, 'his van is a mess and little, so I doubt it, as he can't fit much stock in the back of that van.' My father then made me aware that he was the owner of a company who was the largest supplier of produce to the cruise ships that arrived at Liverpool. My father told me that the owner loved being part of the fruit market, even though he didn't need to be. I was driven around the other side of the market where I would see several large 40ft curtain sider lorries waiting to be loaded, and all had the same company name. I was puzzled why the owner drove an old van. My father stated that he loved that van and had it for around forty years, and that he only uses it when visiting the market, as he wants to feel what it was like when starting off. My father stated that no amount of money can buy certain things, it cannot buy memories, and it cannot turn back time to the days when you started out in business, so the nearest we can do is to buy items from our childhood, that in some small way take us back to those days. I guess this old man was doing just that, as I looked on, it made total sense. I began to admire this person and would ask my dad if he had visited the fruit market when I was not there. I look back now and even miss the days my father would shout at me. I would do anything to spend an afternoon with him, even though I struggle to accept how I was treated differently from my brother. I remember how my dad would always pop his head around the door whilst I trained at the boxing club at a young age. I would shout for him to go away, and now look back hating myself for that. I regret so much; it is hard to not remember the bad things. My father was a funny guy, and he had the ability to make people laugh within seconds. I remember visiting my parents' holiday home with a few different girlfriends, my parents would always be arguing, my mum would shout and swear loudly. The following morning, my dad would always walk to the campsite owner and apologise, saying that it was me and my girlfriend and that he would not allow us to visit again. My mum would be laughing in the caravan and act as though there was nothing wrong with her terrible behaviour. I wanted to learn from my upbringing and do things very differently with how I brought up my children. My wife's words during our wedding whilst she was interviewed always repeat in my mind, she was asked, 'what do you love about him?' she replied, 'I love how he is a good father and how he loves his children.' This was me summed up well, I love my children very much and would do anything for them. I can't help that I was unwell with PTSD when my children were young, all I can do is do my best and try to set the best example I can. I continued to work hard on my home, which now has a large ground floor extension, making it now six rooms on the ground floor and a total of four bedrooms. I have done so much to my home in making it nice and still have many plans with converting it into a five-bedroom house. The house just makes me sad, as it is a family home and deserves a family in it. I often dream of meeting someone, falling in love and having the chance of a family again.

If I had another child, the child would have the most perfect upbringing, as I have a lovely home to offer and all the experience of being a father. I would rather be on my own than be with the wrong person though, and this has been my belief for many years. I am not prepared to settle for anything that I feel is beneath me or wrong for me. I know what I deserve, and I know what I can offer as a good, honest, and loyal man, I will wait for that. I remember my mum's youngest sister once saying to me, 'you can get someone nicer than her', whilst she referred to a girlfriend of mine. I would have been around age fourteen at the time. My auntie was right, as this girl swore a lot and was aggressive. I do feel that during my childhood, the influence my mum's sisters had on me, was a positive one. I have lovely memories of my mum's youngest sister taking me for trainers. My dad would only ever hand over £20, but the Adidas trainers I wanted were called, LA Trainer. I only ever wanted these trainers as one of my favourite cousins from Leigh had them. My auntie would always check if she had spare money to add to the £20, but most of the time she didn't. I would end up buying Adidas Sunny, and the Adidas that didn't have the three little circles in the sole. We would walk around St Johns market and end up in Sayers where my auntie would buy me a cake. We would get the bus home, and I would look at my new trainers on the bus, I can almost still smell that new trainer smell even now.

I would show my dad my new trainers and he would always say the same thing, 'there nice;' and walk away. My dad didn't always hand me £20, at times they had no money, and I would be bought Greenflash, from Asda. I remember running in the street and agreeing with my dad that they made me run faster. I look back and see many differences with me and my dad when it came to being a parent. I have gone many days without food to make sure my son had the trainers he wanted. I am not saying my father didn't have money, but the facts were, he could afford to place a bet on the horses, so he could have afforded to put my trainers first. My mum denies my father gambled on the horses, but I was constantly in the betting office with him whilst he placed a bet. I do admit that the older my father got, the less he betted, and I cannot remember him ever placing a bet from when he reached the age of fifty. I was once given a horse racing tip; it was a tip from a friend of mine who was from Iraq. His grandfather had been some kind of minster in Iraq, I believe. He owned racehorses and so too did his relations. I was given a tip, the horse's name was, Progression. It was 33/1, my dad sent me to the betting office with £35 to place on the horse. It was a short five-furlong race, the horse won with ease. I ran to my dad and handed him all his winnings. It was a perfect time for my parents as they were going on holiday that week. I didn't attend that holiday, as I was thinking about the fun I could have whilst they were away, but now looking back, I get a little upset I didn't join them on all those holidays. We never realise how important a memory is until we lose someone, sadly. I still drive to the conker tree at Knowsley Village and remember how me and my dad would find the biggest sticks to throw up at the conkers. I was there again recently, sadly this was due to visiting my mate's mother, to pay my respects. There has been so many emotions running around me of late, especially with my mate passing recently. It has brought back so many memories from my childhood, and these have mostly involved my dad. I have so many battles when it comes to my father's passing. I must try and accept how I was treated differently, how I was in a way, taken advantage of. My dad would have me drive him around to collect wood for his pigeon sheds, I would help him load and unload and even stack the wood on his land, and only be handed £15 for fuel.

This was during a time my brother was paid a salary for cleaning pigeon sheds and driving the birds for their weekly train. The list is endless with the battles I have, I must try to move on from it all, but I can't right now. I have still not yet visited his grave at Knowsley cemetery. I am aware my sister has been a few times. My young lovely nieces have laid cards and other items for their grandad, but to my disgust they have been removed by someone. I have no idea what kind of evil could remove a young child's items from a grave. I have a battle with wanting to prove my father wrong about me and wanting to make him proud. I am often told that he was proud of my academic achievements, but that is not enough for me, I have so much more to yet prove.

Chapter Thirteen

The Irish Game

Looking back at the days I worked in Irish transport, mostly at the time where I held the role as a regional manager. I would manage my own time, and this was dangerous for me, as I would find it hard to not skive off work. I would have a credit card with a huge balance to wine and dine customers. I would always have a morning and afternoon meeting booked, but at times, and especially if visiting a beautiful location. I would rearrange the afternoon appointment to the morning. I would finish the two morning appointments by 11 a.m. and have the rest of the day to myself. I would pop along to a few country pubs and enjoy an afternoon meal. I would get talking to the locals, and they would be fascinated by the job I did. I would have to order two meals, as it would then appear from the receipt that I was taking a customer out for a meeting. People would often look across and probably think I was very greedy, as I ordered two of everything. I was very aware that the owner was taking advantage of me at times by not paying me the correct amount of commission owed, so this was my way to play the same game as him. These afternoons out would often turn into little adventures, especially when I had to drive a long distance from home. It would be common for me to drive to London on a weekly basis. I would always still find the time to drive my children to school most days, but during London trips it was impossible. I would attend meetings, and often not even talk about haulage, instead get onto private chats about life and hobbies.

I would talk for hours at times with clients who would tell me about their private lives and where they enjoyed holidaying. I loved my job, but it was boring at times, and it could be very stressful. I was very unwell still with PTSD at this time and it did affect my work. I found it hard to concentrate and would often lose interest in winning work and instead, I would skive off, usually to a country park. I would end up sitting on a bench for hours daydreaming. I would often sit and place bets on my phone, wasting money that should have benefited my children's future, this was the issue being so well paid. I always knew another large pay check would be on its way at the end of that month. There were some scary moments when working in Irish transport. I remember visiting a large company at Cheetham Hill, Manchester. My director wanted this business a lot, as it fitted in with the routes we took in Ireland. They must have shipped around thirteen full loads a week. I turned up for the meeting, and was instantly confronted by three large Asian males, who informed me that this was an Asian area and that any Irish business is not wanted, they also told me to fuckoff. These Asian men either owned or represented the transport firm who was currently handling all the traffic. I drove away and informed my director what had happened. I was called the following day; I heard a northern Irish voice on the phone that I didn't recognise asking me what had gone on the previous day. This male told me that him and his fellows secretly own a share of the company I worked for and that it is in his interest that the business does well. I was told to describe the men who approached me and what company they came from. The voice sounded scary in a way, as I could tell that this male meant business. The call ended without providing me any further instructions, so I continued with my work as usual, but a week later I received a call again from the same male. His Irish voice was calm, but still scary for some reason. He told me to return to the Cheetham Hill company for another meeting and that this time there will not be any bother. I set up the meeting and returned, I won the business that day, but as I walked out of the building, to my shock the three Asian men were standing waiting to meet me at the rear of the building. It would be very easy for them to attack me and probably get away with it, so it was a scary experience. They looked at me and smiled, saying, 'we had no idea who you are with, we are sorry for last week, this is for you, have a good day, mate,' They handed me a bottle of whisky, it was Scottish. I was unsure whether they were being funny when knowing we are an Irish company. or just not aware that it was Scottish whisky. I called up my director and told him what had happened. He was happy that I got the business, and he told me to continue with my week, but I couldn't resist asking him who the other Irish male was. He replied, 'mid 80's I was forced to borrow money from an organisation, but in return they would be silent partners.' A year passed and I knew that the business was not doing too well. I was called by my director who informed me that a group of Irish males will attend the depot and take away nine of the cabs, as they were sold. A cab is the name we give to the front of a lorry, the part that pulls the trailer. Each cab had to be worth around £30,000. Two white Ford transits vans turned up at the depot and a group of men got out. They were not big men, only average, but scary and intimidating. I would rather be in a fight against a large man who takes steroids than one of those average, Irish men. I could see that they were tough, they didn't appear to be businessmen. A few hours passed and one of the drivers drove into the yard, he was an Irish driver from Belfast. He asked me if the cabs had been taken, and I made him aware of what had happened. He asked me if I knew who they were, which I didn't, he laughed saying, you no idea who they were? He went onto say, if only you knew who they were and walked away. I couldn't believe that the company I worked for appeared to be part owned by such a group. It wasn't long before the company closed, I was owed six weeks' pay and some commission, I didn't receive it either, so I kept the BMW car, which had to be worth around £30,000. I was not prepared to hand it back until I got the pay that was owed to me, a few weeks went by, and one late evening the car was taken from my drive. I didn't even report it stolen, as it was clear who had taken it. I had a few thousand in the bank at this time, so I would enjoy my time off work and spend as much time with my children as I could. I missed working in Irish transport, and I could write a book on my experience. We had one customer named, John. He would never tell me his address, as it would be different delivery drops each time. He once had four full loads getting delivered to an address just outside Cork. He refused to give me his address, even saying to me, 'I am sick of you asking for my details you nosey scouse bastard.' It was madness, as the drivers on the day of delivery had no idea where they were going. The only instructions we were given was to take a main road, which was many miles long and as good as the length of an English motorway. I received a call that day informing me that there was a young boy sat on the roadside with a chair and a pack lunch holding a sign which read, 'John Paints.' The customer had this poor young boy sat at the roadside for six hours waiting to flag down the wagons. This would only ever happen in Ireland, I feel. The same owner was pulled up at Lymm services in Cheshire when he was asked by police for his driving license and papers for the hazardous paint he was carrying. This crazy the Irishman replied, 'I am from Ireland, and we don't need your fucking license or papers, we are not under your law, as I am only visiting here for a few hours.' I honestly believe that he believed that madness he spoke that day. The police seized his vehicle and took him away in the police car. I have no idea what happened to him that day, as I would not hear from that customer again. The funniest one for me, was when a depot manager called me asking for me to call a customer, as 4,000 euros was owed. I called the customer who stated, 'It is your lucky day, you are getting 500 euros and a chance to stay at my holiday home on the coast for free for a whole week at no cost.' I asked him what the hell was he talking about. You would get to meet the craziest people, but it was all fun and laughs. Working with the Irish has been the best working experience I have had to date, they are the nicest people I have ever met. I am proud that my name, and my mum's maiden name are both Northern Irish names. The only bad memories that I have whilst working in Irish Transport, are the days I suffered with my PTSD. I would shake at times when hearing loud bangs. I wouldn't even think about the shooting. I guess my body, would instantly remember the trauma. I would become nervous, even look around for quick escape routes, and would have no idea why I was doing it. I would end up frustrated and upset, going home moody. It destroyed so much my PTSD.I am so glad that today it is almost fully gone from my life. I can understand why some people who have experienced war, as an example, will always suffer in some way, and I guess I will do too in a way. Not seeing my children also caused PTSD. I get upset whenever I think about the times I didn't see them. I made many friends in Ireland and stayed in touch with most of them. I would speak with friends during the time I didn't see my children and I would be given words of encouragement that all would be okay. I was very tempted to work in Ireland and move across for a year or two, but the thought of living a distance from my children was too much for me to handle. I turned down three job offers to stay in the industry. I would have been well paid, but I simply could not move across to

Ireland. The companies that I had worked for, had offices based in England and so do the companies who offered me roles, but they wanted me to live in Ireland for the first nine months of the job role. Being jobless was okay at first, but I soon became bored. I started to miss the driving to destinations in England and Ireland that I had not been before, it was like an adventure when working in Irish Transport. I would have meetings daily and never know where I was going most of the time. I would drive around admiring the view, and as stated skive off work to a few countryside pubs. I was now stuck at home; and this would not do my mental health any good. I was still married when I came out of Irish Transport and that was what led to the decline of my marriage. It was probably already long over at this stage, but me stuck at home speeded up the separation process. I became lazy and would often sleep until late morning; my fitness was also declining. I was under the impression at the time that I could always get a job back in transport without an issue. I also convinced myself that I needed a few months off work. It was now 2014, leading up to February, this was the month my wife left me. I ended up being off work for just over a year, and now that my wife had left me, I was not motivated to gain employment, but something inside me was shouting for me to fight, to get up and be a man, reminding me that I am a father who needs to set the right example. I applied for a few roles and was lucky enough to gain a role back in transport. It was out of my comfort zone, as it was dedicated English haulage. This meant I had to try and rebuild a customer database, as the customers I knew mainly dealt with Irish traffic. This new company only wanted work out of Manchester, which made it even more difficult. I was getting on well on this new role, but six months passed, and I started to feel I was back earning good money, sadly this would all end at speed. I was driving into work on the M62 motorway, I came to a stop due to traffic ahead, when suddenly a car smashed into the rear of my car. I was thrown forwards and badly hurt my back and neck areas. I was forced to go off work sick for a period of six months. Work was constantly pressurising me to go back, but I was far to unwell. I started a personal injury claim which resulted in over £6,000 compensation. I needed this money, as work dismissed me the week, I was due to go back, this put me back to square one. The money from my claim did help me survive, it also helped me create a business plan. I started a landscaping business; I purchased thousands of leaflets which would get me some work. I visited an accountant to make sure that all I was doing was correct, this removed stress, as I was thinking I was making errors with my accounts. It was much easier to pass it all onto an accountant, the fee wasn't that much per year either. Eighteen months passed and during these eighteen months I had gone on countless holidays and weekends away with my wife who I was separated from. I was totally unaware that during this period that she had met someone and started an affair. If I had known, I would not have gone on those holidays with her. The moment I found out about the affair. I didn't take it well. I sent approximately forty text messages of abuse, which resulted in my ex-wife being awarded a non-molestation order. This restricted me from contacting her, which was hard, as I needed to see my children. She started to keep the children from seeing me and looking back I am now aware she was only taking advice from her legal adviser at the time. It was all feeling so very wrong, as I never assaulted anyone, threatened anyone, or damaged any property. I was just upset at finding out about the affair. I am far from innocent when it came to an affair, as there was one occasion I kissed a female client from work, we went back to her place, and I stayed for a few hours. She wanted to start a relationship with me, but I completely ignored her. She found out I was with someone when she called my office at work asking for me and was told that I was off work with maternity leave. I have never forgiven myself for that night with the female. I ended it straight away, as my wife at the time and children were far too important. The first breach of the non-molestation order occurred when attending my ex-wife's home asking her what the forms were. I was made to carry out community hours, but thankfully, at the appeal, the judge removed those hours. The second breach also involved community hours. I was ordered to work at a charity shop packing clothes. I was recognised from an old client who I knew when working in Irish transport. I had to say that I was volunteering for the charity shop, as it caused embarrassment. I was struggling with money and would hardly eat at times. I was having to pay legal fees, which took all my savings from me, which was over £10,000 at that time. I was starting to get some work in with the business. However, whatever I earned I needed to pay legal fees and court costs., so I was working for free in a way, and for nearly five years in total. It was my third week at the charity shop, and I was asked to work with a steam machine for the first time. The machine was old, and the rear of the shop had no room, it was dangerous to use such a machine, but I was pressured into carrying out the duty. The lady at the charity wasn't nice at all and would often threaten to report you to probation. The steam machine made a huge banging noise and squirted boiling water all over my arm and hand. I was in a lot of pain, and there were no taps working at the shops for me to run my arm through cold running water. I had to leave early and made my way to the A&E department at Warrington hospital. That week I visited the solicitors who informed me that I could claim against the probation service due to the machine being old and the working conditions dangerous. I was again awarded a sum of money for a personal injury, which made me accept the fact that I was having to carry out the community hours, as I was now in a way being paid to work. People laughed when I would say, yes, I worked, but got paid well for them hours, as I was awarded over £7,000 compensation. I needed that money at the time, as I was struggling badly and had even missed my mortgage payments for the previous two months. I was now able to get up to date with all my household bills. I was eighteen months into having a business at this stage, which was all going well. I was just sad and always upset, as whenever I earned money, I was forced to transfer it to solicitors that represented me, or my ex-wife's solicitor, or to my ex-wife. The debt was never ending, but I reminded myself that if I could pay it all and keep the family home, I knew I would end up in a better position, and I would be able to do what is best for my children. The kids had been through so much and they needed a home that was familiar to them, and the only home they knew was the main family home. I was disgusted that my ex-wife tried to force sell the house and even more disgusted that her solicitor laughed in court looking at me whilst saying, 'the husband will walk away with £19,000.' They applied to have me evicted from my own home, which was never going to happen in a court of law. It was clear my ex-wife's solicitor was providing terrible and false advice. The idea they had was, to down value the home and sell it fast. My legal advisor at the time also had a belief that they may have the idea of trying to buy me out, as they stated the house was worth much less than it was. Thankfully, the court requested independent valuations, which clearly demonstrated the house was worth a lot more than my ex-wife stated. I got more work and made more payments to my ex-wife. I was slightly short on one occasion, and I was taken back to court due to not paying all. I promised to pay it, just two months after the date previously agreed. The court awarded me more time but made me pay over

£8,700 in legal fees to my ex-wife's solicitor. My ex-wife was blind to the fact that her solicitor was clearly provoking legal fees. This behaviour was not in the best interests of our children and that was what upset me most. I have only ever done what is in the best interest of the children. My ex-wife was only following her legal advice, and I am sure that she thought she was doing what was best at the time. I would always think that I should have gone to Ireland, as I would have been earning good money, and would have cleared the debt at speed. I look back today thankful I didn't go, as getting to see my eldest son after football helped him and that is worth more to me than any amount of money. I received a call out the blue, towards the end of 2023. It was from an old Irish haulage firm that I use to deal with. He was asking me how I was getting on and what I was up to. I couldn't believe he still had my number. He had opened a depot just outside London and wanted someone to run it. He stated that he had always admired me and wanted me to work for him for some time. I explained to him all I had been through and that I have a duty as a father to stay here for my children, especially now that my eldest son had moved in with me. I will always miss the Irish transport game, and I will especially miss working with the Irish. They are the greatest people in the world for me, and I am very proud to have the Irish roots I have. I intend exploring more of Ireland one day soon with my children.

Chapter Fourteen

Reflection

I often sit for hours at a time reflecting on my life. I think how it went wrong, how I messed up relationships, and how I messed up opportunities that were offered to me on plate. I met a decent girl from Stockport, but this was just eighteen months after I separated from my wife. I was not in the right frame of mind for a relationship, but I continued with it, which I regret, as that girl was amazing and didn't deserve to be upset by a man who was a walking wreck. I even attended Christmas dinner with this girl and met her family. This day turned out to be a disaster, as during the afternoon. I went to use the toilet; I used far too much tissue paper and blocked the toilet. I also jammed the door shut. I was far too scared to force the door, as my girlfriend would have already been very angry with me for using so much toilet paper, especially after constantly warning me not to use too much toilet paper. I tried to look out of the window, but to my shock there were two police officers standing outside, with German shepherd dogs. I was unaware at this moment that a married couple who were both police officers lived next door. They looked at me wondering what the hell I was doing. I went back inside the bathroom and put my full arm down the toilet and managed to unblock it. I then got near naked to wash myself, as I felt disgusted after placing my arm into the toilet. If anyone would have come into the toilet at that moment, I dread to think what they would have thought. I managed to force the door open and walk back to the living area as though all was okay. My girlfriend immediately looked at me frowning, as she knew I had been up to something. I enjoyed visiting New Mills, it is a lovely place. I am saddened looking back that it never worked out with that girl, it was another example of how I ruined things when it came to a good relationship. I would have a habit of meeting someone at the wrong time, I was not mentally right to start a relationship when I did, just as I was not mentally stable to get my ex-wife pregnant when I did. This is the problem with so many people, they jump into a relationship damaged or mentally unwell. We all deserve a stable person who has all their affairs together, as well as their state of mind, sadly, all that is lacking today. Most of my reflections are sad memories. I would look back at the negative experiences where I messed up in life, rather than any success I had. It was April 2023, and I noticed that I started to have leaking from a very small hole near the rear of my backside. The GP surgery didn't see anything, but I knew that something was not right, so I popped to the hospital. It was confirmed that I was suffering from a fistula, and surgery would be needed. I was very much alone at this stage of my life, so I was panicking how I would get to and from the hospital. The hospital informed me that they will not discharge me unless I have someone to pick me up after surgery. My sister agreed to get me after surgery, but she was busy on that day, and without any notice I had to think on my feet. I had to lie to the nurse by stating that my eldest son was picking me up his car, when in fact it was an Uber driver taking me home. I waited outside the hospital alone when I suddenly became dizzy, falling to the ground. It was the side effects from the general anaesthetic. I wanted to call my sister but knew she was busy with her children, so I walked back inside to the hospital where nurses came to my aid. I waited inside for an hour, before arranging a second Uber driver to come and collect me.

The nurse asked me if that was a different car outside, I said, 'no, that's my son, 'Thankfully she didn't notice that the driver was an Asian male who clearly wasn't my son. I got into the car, and we drove home, I walked into the house and immediately went to bed, as the dizzy spells came back once more. The following day I was very upset, as it hit me once more that I had no one in my life and no one appeared to care for me either. My children knew I had surgery and didn't call to see how I was, and their mother didn't bring them to see me either. It was only my eldest son who spoke with me on the phone after I called him. He was willing to get the bus straightaway to see me, which would have been a big journey for him from university, I told him I was okay, but it made me proud that he was willing to make the journey. The day after getting from hospital, would just stay in bed for most of the day, imagining that my grandmother was sat beside me, telling me that all would be okay and that there is nothing to worry about. I started to recover after a week, I was working in the call centre at this stage of my life but would soon again be forced to go off work sick. Six months passed from the operation, and I again noticed that there was something not right at the top of my right leg. There was a large lump, it was the size of an apple. I was still speaking to my female friend at the time, she was good enough to get her daughter minded and she popped across to see me. She examined the lump and agreed that we needed to go to the hospital. I was extremely thankful; that she joined me to the hospital. I was growing feelings for this person and even more so now that she was helping me whilst I was needing help, but I knew it would not go anywhere, which was a constant battle when considering if it would work with her. She waited for nine hours with me that day, right up to the point it was concluded that I have an internal abscess. The male junior doctor had no one else examine me that day and so he discharged me with antibiotics, informing me that I will receive a call Thursday of that week. I near passed out on the way home, and when getting home things didn't improve. I was shaking in the middle of the night and sweating badly. My t-shirt was soaking with the sweat pouring from me. The days passed, and I became worse at speed, I had my son on the Sunday that approached. The hospital had no record of a call planned for Thursday, which annoyed me. I needed to go back to the hospital, I got another lift from my female friend, and she waited with me again. I was examined and told by a senior doctor that I should not have gone home, she explained that urgent surgery is needed to drain the abscess. I could have died from septicaemia, that junior doctor should never have allowed me to leave the hospital that week. I waited for ten hours before being given a private room, and even then, I would wait another twenty hours before I would be sent to surgery. I woke up after surgery and called my auntie to see if anyone could provide me a lift home. My auntie did pop into the hospital that day, it was lovely seeing her. I was very upset that my mum didn't call once to see how her son was, and she would have been told by my auntie that I was in hospital. No one called me to see how I was, but my female friend was there yet again to drive me home and look after me. The fistula healed by itself, but I was told that it may reoccur, and a check-up will be needed in six months' time. I was becoming more and more worried about health issues, especially after losing my father. I needed to be healthy for my children and wanted to watch them succeed in life. I wanted to make sure I would always be there for them, offering support. Having surgery twice in proximity was a huge wake up call. I started to pay close attention to my diet and fitness levels. I began running daily and would start fasting each week. I would often go many months with no alcohol, and I could feel the benefits. My sleep improved, also my memory, and I wasn't tired throughout the day. I was still in the habit of wanting to escape and would often check into a hotel in Liverpool at the end of each month. I would only stay at a hotel two nights, but it was enough for me to feel that I had escaped from my life. Escaping to a hotel was a great way for me to reflect on life. I would often sit at the Albert Dock for hours at a time going through my mistakes. I don't want to beat myself up too much, as I was not always to blame for my relationships failing. I was certainly to blame for my marriage failing and that was the big loss in my life. There were two other relationships that failed after my marriage, I could not be blamed for these relationships failing. They were both toxic girls, but saying that, I was starting to fall in love with one of them. She moved into my home at speed, and she had a lovely family. She just couldn't be trusted, as she had many issues. She was taking drugs on a regular basis, but you would not think that looking at her. She was a mess when it came to the friendships she had developed. Her friends were using her in all kinds of ways, even her female friends. They were lingering around, and I dread to think what for. She had the worst group of friends, the lowest of the low, and as the saying goes, 'you become like your friends.' The other female was my worst ever experience to date when it came to a relationship. She was violent and aggressive; she had a drink problem and would often drink until she was drunk. She was a very attractive girl and again you would not think she had any issues looking at her. She did not have the nicest of families, they were vile people. I was even sent messages from fake accounts from her family members, mostly from one disgusting sister of hers after we split. She threatened to kidnap and rape my daughter, and this was not a good move with me, as I would die for my daughter. They were trying to get a reaction looking back and would never have tried such a move. I contacted the police who were a waste of time, as Cheshire police force wanted to pass it to Merseyside and Merseyside wanted to pass it back. It was a sickening display from the police at the time. This girl was constantly jealous of my ex-wife for some reason, and I would constantly be accused of still being in love with my ex-wife. The relationship ended due to two terrible nights, which involved a great deal of violence. We were out drinking during the first incident, we stopped at a graveyard and began talking, as per usual the topic of my ex-wife would be brought up. I was sitting against a tree when out of the blue, she pushed my head hard against the tree. The back of my head hit the tree and began to bleed. I was dizzy, I grabbed her and pushed her back, as I needed to defend myself from her jealous outburst. She then grabbed a concrete pot from one of the graves and swung it hard, hitting my face, which knocked out my tooth. My mouth was bleeding heavily, and I fell to the ground. I could see her running away at speed, leaving me laying on the ground bleeding. I took pictures of my face and videoed the blood spiling from my face. I managed to make it home that night, and the next morning I went back to the graveyard to look for my tooth. I have no idea why, I just had it in my head that the tooth could be saved. I was brushing through the tree leaves when I heard my name being called. She had returned and asked if I needed help to look for my tooth. I couldn't believe that we were both now looking for my tooth, we both looked a mess. We hadn't washed and were both wearing the same clothes from the evening before. I had dried blood on my face and a swollen lip. We managed to find the tooth, I wanted to see if it would go back into my mouth, but the tooth had now changed colour, it appeared grey.

I went home and we both thought of what we could do. I painted the tooth with white deluxe paint and placed it into my mouth. My crazy girlfriend looked at me and began laughing hysterically, saying that it is extremely bright in colour. I even got my hand grinder out at one point and tried to cut and shape the tooth. It was clear I was facing a hopeless task, so I gave up and attended the dentist where it was concluded that I would now need an implant if wanting a tooth in its place. There were many crazy evenings involving this person, especially when she got drunk, So many occasions she would walk into a garden of a house we passed, she would lay down and start to fall asleep. This relationship was not healthy and if anything, it was extremely dangerous, as this person was clearly very unwell and would often change personality at speed. We started a business together and rented a small office in the area that I lived. I was very honest and open with her about the takings and outgoings of the business, but she still accused me of taking money, even though I counted the takings in front of her. She was very aware of what takings we made that day, as it was her carrying out the treatments. I would always dread the end of the day when we had that business, I would become very nervous, as I waited for a verbal attack of some form. The second incident was the incident that ended the relationship. We were out at the local pub when I received an email from my ex-wife. I looked at the email and smiled with sarcasm, as it was relating to the divorce that was active at that stage. My girlfriend looked at me with fire in her eyes, asking me who the email was from. I made her aware, and she immediately asked me why I was smiling. I knew what was coming up, and I couldn't be dealing with it on this day, as I was tired. I told her that I was smiling because I was still in love with my ex-wife.

I stated this sarcastically, as it must have been what she wanted to hear, as whenever I stated something else, such as the truth, I would be attacked. She immediately punched me in my face, and I left the pub, as she chased after me, she fell on the steps and broke her fingernail. She then shouted at me, accusing me of causing the broken nail. I ran home as fast as I could. She turned up at my home screaming outside and threatening to smash my windows. I called the police, the moment the police turned up, she moved away from my front door and sat on the curb side. The male officer asked me what had happened. I invited him into my home, and we spoke in a civilised manner, but a few moments later a disgusting aggressive female office came towards my home shouting at me and accusing me of breaking my girlfriend's fingernail. I made her aware that I had been punched in the face, but the female officer arrested me for assault. My girlfriend was rotten drunk and looked a mess, her hair was sticking up and her makeup dripping. They took her back to the police station and took pictures of her in that state. It may appear that she had been attacked, when this simply was not the case, she was just a mess from being drunk and falling when chasing after me as she left the pub. I was taken to the police station and provided an interview. I simply told the truth and highlighted that the pub would have cameras, which will show me being punched. The landlady at the time knew that there were lots of people dealing and taking drugs in that pub, so she stated to the police the cameras were not working, when they were. It was still okay, as several witnesses came forward. I was also approached by two neighbours who lived at the rear of the road, who witnessed her chasing after me. It was now the following morning, and I had been in a police cell for twenty hours. I was released without any charge, as my girlfriend withdrew her drunken statement, even if the statement was made the following morning.

She would have still been slightly drunk due to the amount that she drank on that terrible evening. The police didn't even give me a lift home, even though I was nine miles from home. I had to walk for several hours to get home, I was feeling so very beat up. I was fed up with life at this point, as I had gone through so much. The divorce and not seeing my children was so tough on me. This experience was the last thing I needed, and it was a relief to see that the girl had met someone at speed, who I assume she must have been talking to whilst with me. This was a learning experience, and I had to take on board all what happened during those two terrible relationships. I needed to avoid girls who were trouble, which is easier said than done, as these days people are very good at appearing to be normal and in a good frame of mind, when in fact, a lot of people are damaged and have lots of issues. There is a perception that it is only men who commit physical abuse, when in fact many women are also guilty of such. Reflecting on relationships is a good thing, you need to know where it went wrong, or why that person was not suited to you. It is important when you plan children, or if your partner becomes pregnant that you are well suited. I feel far too many people today relationship hop, and that is why I decided to stay single for long periods. I wanted to learn more about who I am and what I wanted from a relationship. The negative with being single is that it would allow me to reflect on my life, which would at times cause me to be upset due to the many lost opportunities. I had become a lot more self-aware, and I feel that was down to my studies. When you are studying law, you are constantly reading case law. I would always try and see why the judge set the principles in landmark cases, and it always made sense to me after examining the details. I noticed that I started to use these studying techniques when living day to day life.

I would stand back more, analysing my behaviour and looking at the situation from a neutral standpoint. I would start to notice my issues and address them when I could. I knew I needed to change in many ways and one can only do this if one knows what needs changing. When I attended the course that was recommended by the family court, so many of the young men didn't appear to have any self-awareness, they could see no wrong in what they did and would immediately pass the blame. There were some men who were treated badly by the system, like me. There are so many issues with the system, I doubt it will ever improve completely. The probation service doesn't appear to be monitored, as it is privately run in most areas. I attended court due to a breach of the probation conditions and even the judges stated that he was aware of the issues with the probation service. I presented the evidence showing that I had texted the probation service, making them aware I was working that day and even showing the court I had a reply stating that it was okay and to just turn up the following week. I was then handed a breach for not turning up for the previous appointment that was agreed to be cancelled. I complained, the probation officer was disgusting who investigated the matter, and no shock as he was dating the female probation officer assigned to me. These details were repeated many times to the court and other departments and each time it fell on deaf ears. It was clear that I had developed a hatred towards the system, and I wanted to go to war with it. I had so much anger in me due to how I had been treated and lied to. The biggest upset I had was the fact it was due to the system that I was not seeing my children for a fourteen-month period. I needed to calm the temper inside me and instead play the game more intelligently. I wanted to grow from the experience and learn from it, but sadly, we mostly only ever learn from bad experiences.

They either make you or break you, and many had tried previously to break me and failed. The many schools, the unit, and even the army failed to break me. I have a good mixture of friends who I have known over the years, and many have been through bad times. I would always look at those friends and see how they responded to bad experiences. Some men walk around for the rest of their lives full of hate and anger, but some grow from a bad experience. They learn and develop as a man; this then attracts only good things towards you. The ones who developed all seem to meet good partners and have good careers, but the ones full of hate appeared to be struggling constantly with their lives. I always had my father's advice at the forefront of my mind, and that was to keep my bills up to date and work hard. If I continued to do this, I would attract only good towards me. I was still failing in many areas of my life, as my attitude would let me down regularly, but on a positive note, I would always notice such and write down my errors, making a point of addressing such. It is only you who can change you at times, I feel. People can try and force the issue, but this only ever causes one to then battle and go to war with others or oneself. My parents beat me weekly, well into my teens as they tried to force change. The army and the schools also served me with punishments. This only caused me to resist and fight back, as it made me feel that everyone was going to war with me rather than helping me. I look back now and realise that many schools, including the army were totally unaware how to get the best out of a young man. People perform better when they feel better, and I personally responded better to a more civilised approach. This is why I didn't misbehave with teachers who appeared to take time out in talking to you about what the issue is.

I wanted to be totally different as a parent to what my parents were with me. I listened to my children more, and I took on board what they said. I still made errors as I have admitted, but my children have never been afraid to speak out and tell me off in a way. My youngest son would often tell me that I need to change at times, he would tell me that I had caused embarrassment in certain situations. It is not about if he is right or wrong, it's about how he feels and how he has perceived the incidents. I needed to reflect on how he saw me as a man, as I want my children to be proud of me. University has helped me more than anything else when it came to self-awareness. Today I am constantly analysing myself, even writing down areas that I need to improve on, and even how I would feel during certain stressful matters. A diary is so much more that a diary at times, it allows you to look back, It allows you to recall how you felt in certain situations and how you reacted. I also noted down how my diet was going, as your diet and alcohol consumption plays a big role with how and who you are as a man. I was becoming a better man each day and starting to like who I was. I have liked who I am since 2019. It can be a tough journey in getting to like who you are, as it takes a lot of change at times.

Chapter Fifteen

Craving to improve

The one thing I had started to notice about myself from the year 2019 is that I craved to want to change for the better. I wanted to become the best version of myself that was possible. I had a good heart and always wanted to help others when I could. I would still pop the shops with any spare money and buy flowers. I would then hand the flowers out to strangers on the street. I would also always keep a look out for any volunteering work that was advertised. My CV was starting to look impressive, but there were a lot of courses highlighted relating to children, and it was clear that this is one area I would struggle with due to the civil breaches on my DBS. I was aware that the breaches would fall off after eleven years, but this meant I had to wait until 2028 for the convictions to be removed, and by that time I would be much older, probably past the age of wanting to start a new career. It is difficult to find a career that suits you best. We all have an urge for a different job, and we always compare ourselves to other people. I simply wanted to continue improving as a man, and wanted to send out a message in the hope that others could learn from my story. There is nothing good about being shot, hanging out with tough men, or climbing through windows naked. The list is endless when it comes my negative experiences. I wanted to make sure that my story doesn't promote bad behaviour and instead demonstrates that getting involved with the wrong crowd, or even being near certain environments only leads to negative outcomes.

If you go somewhere where there is likely to be trouble and you get into trouble, then it is your own fault. This statement gets repeated in my mind repeatedly at times. I text my boys the same message, but thankfully they are well behaved and do not resemble me as a youngster, which is a good thing. I want my message that change is a good thing, the want to improve and become a better man is a good message to spread. There are so many youngsters out there who think it is funny to be mixed up in negative behaviour or think it's a good thing to be mixing with the wrong crowd. We are all guilty of thinking we have more time than what we have. As youngsters, we behave as though we live until three hundred years of age. If only youngsters realised how little time, we all have, and the limited time that we all have in achieving the goals that we may create for ourselves. Time is so precious, and very limited, and as an example. If one wants to achieve a PHD, they need to attend college, university, post graduate degree and a PHD. This process is a minimum of seven years. I could have achieved this at a young age, but here I am in my 40s and only now starting the process. Youngsters have no idea just how much is available for them at school, college, and university, but sadly, so many youngsters feel that university is out of reach for them. This can be down to bad parenting or growing up in deprived negative areas. They look around, only seeing negative, then accept that they are part of that environment, and that it is also their future. When in fact, they can escape the environment and improve; everyone is capable of anything if putting their minds to it. Making youngsters feel better is key, I feel. Giving them confidence and repeatedly telling them that they can achieve whatever they want. University is easy enough to get into if they want it.

My eldest son struggled at secondary school, but he put his mind to it and achieved a grade of distinction at college and now attends university. He doesn't speak about his journey much, but I am sure there were times he didn't think it was possible. I am aware that my father contacted his sister at one point, as he wanted to offer some form of support for her children. My dad's sister has always been in trouble with the police and has been in and out of prison. We adopted one of the girls, but my dad's sister has approximately ten children in total. A year after my father passed, I learnt that one of the twin girls had been fostered by my cousin, but my cousin couldn't take her on fully due to how busy she was with her own children. This meant that the young girl would be thrown back into the system. This played on my mind a lot, as I had experienced so much when shadowing barristers who worked in child protection. It made me upset thinking about the twins, and how they must be affected by the different living environments. I wanted to track them down, but my cousin provided little information, so I needed to do the hard work myself. I contacted several local authorities, but each time I struggled, as I had very little information. I didn't even know what prison my auntie was at, so I had to write to several prisons with the hope of her getting back to me. A few months passed when I received a text message out of the blue from one of the twins. This made me so happy, and I immediately made her aware that I am family and there for any support that she may need. I offered to take them out for a meal and even buy them trainers. I am hoping that I can build a relationship with them over the coming years, so that I can always be there for them when needed. I started to create activities in my life, activities that would help me continue to improve as a man.

I was praying much more and reading more of the bible, this was providing me a lot of comfort. It is hard at times when you are alone, so having your religion with you can make you feel you have support in other ways. You also feel that any good you do, doesn't go unnoticed. I started to like me more and more, and I knew I was on track to becoming the best version of myself. I would wake up each morning full of energy, and wanting to spread the word, make youngsters aware of my experience and how it damaged my progress, how it delayed me achieving, and prevented a career in law at a young age. I wanted to share my story with how it didn't benefit me hanging out with the wrong crowd and being around nightclubs every weekend. It is okay to have some friends who are into the night life, and as stated, the lads from Runcorn were good lads, especially the brothers who I got to know.

As I look back over my life, I can see all the mistakes that I have made, it is all now so very clear. What annoys me the most is, all those mistakes could have been very easily avoided. I completed more child mentor courses and applied for more volunteer work. I wanted to not just improve as a man but improve in every way possible. I always made sure my garden was neat and tidy, so too the house. I ordered new carpets and had the house decorated throughout. I was mopping the floors daily, and make sure my bed was made each morning. My bedding was washed every four days, and I also kept on top of my clothes too. I was turning into a well-oiled machine, developing a healthy routine for my mind and body. I still had no female in my life, but by this time I had developed a strong independent mind, which didn't need anyone unless it was someone who would benefit my life, and I would also benefit theirs.

The negative I had at this point, was that I continued to beat myself up, and almost daily at times. I cannot forget the mistakes I had made and the time I had wasted. I also could never forgive myself for causing the breakdown of my marriage. I was in debt to my children for breaking up their family home environment, this debt will hang over me for the rest of my life. This is why I am constantly giving my children everything I have; I have gone without food multiple times to make sure my children had what they asked for. The one big challenge I have had, is trying to put to aside the upset I have towards my ex-wife and for how she deceived me, making me pay for so many weekends and holidays away whilst she was seeing another man. She knew I would never have gone on holiday if knowing about the affair, but if I wanted to completely change and become a better person. I had to put those feelings to one side and remind myself that this woman is the mother of my children. It is their mother and that is something I needed to respect. I also wanted to set the correct example before my boys and show them how a real man behaves. This is why I have always jumped to my ex-wife's needs. If she has ever asked me for anything I have gone running to provide it. I made sure my boys had gifts for every Mother's Day and birthday. On a few occasions I have received nothing for Father's Day, but if I then did the same in return, who wins? What example does that set to my boys? If I don't get presents for Father's Day, that is not my issue, that is other people's problem. Two wrongs do not make a right and I need to break the chain, and the way of doing that is to always do what is right no matter what happens in return. I was even emailed on one occasion making me aware that my youngest son will not be bringing his new trainers across or coat, and that I must supply my son with trainers for when he is with me.

This was one subject that would upset me a lot, as I will not allow my son to live in that manner. I emailed disagreeing and that I will not allow for my son to have different clothes for when he visits different parents, thankfully, it has never been an issue since, as me and my son's mum now agree in this area. I was asked by my youngest son if he could take his new Xbox Series to his mums that I bought him, he also asked the same with the laptop I got him, and many other items. I always responded with the same statement, 'The items are not mine son, they belong to you, and you can, and must do whatever you want with them, so take them were you want and do whatever pleases you.' I have read a few times on social media how parents post comments with how they disagree, or how they would stop their children taking items to the other parents' home. I find it very childish behaviour that would only ever be damaging to the children who are stuck in the middle of it all. I struggled not attending the parents' evening as a family, yes, I am aware we are no longer married, but I just feel that parents should attend together, as this shows a togetherness. It demonstrates that the parents are working together in the best interest of the child. Since our separation, sadly, we have only attended the school parents' evening once together. This does disappointment me, but I must not take it to heart and instead, except that's how it is. I am aware my ex-wife works extremely hard in making sure that the schoolwork is up to date, and I am very thankful for all the hard work she has done with the children. The proof is in the pudding, my eldest two are both at university, so she must do a lot right. I have noticed that I am starting to react differently more and more, but I am still far from perfect. A young male screamed at me only last week, swearing and threatening me for no reason, just because he thought I pulled in front of him. Road rage is a terrible thing, and it was something I did almost daily when I suffered with PTSD.

I did respond to the male with the words, 'fuck off.' I reflected on that incident when I got home, and I addressed my behaviour. I thought how tense I got when shouting those words back, and how it made me feel. I didn't feel good and for several hours I was feeling regret and anger towards myself for responding to the aggression towards me. My father would always walk away and turn his cheek. It is hard to do it at times, but it is the correct course of action. Why allow some bad people to upset your day, making you swear, shout, and react. It is allowing the incident to turn you into them in a way, you become like the aggressor. If you smile and forget those kinds of people, you continue with your day as normal. The opposite wins most of the time, water puts out fire, fighting fire with fire will only create a bigger issue. I believe that we are all tested daily in some way, and the less we react, the stronger we become. I started to feel that I was creating more with my life. I wanted to travel as much as possible, nothing was holding me back. I just constantly thought that any holidays or travel should include my children. I do feel that what you experienced as a youngster, is how you will want to be as an adult and parent. My childhood involved a large family going on holiday and I have some lovely memories. I just wanted my children to have the same memories, but when you are divorced, it becomes a very different way of living. I was given back the rings when we separated, which was upsetting as it made me feel that they meant nothing to my ex-wife. I spent a lot of money on the rings and knew that they had value. I was struggling so many times when I studied and during my five years divorce. I did pop to a pawnbroker, who made me aware that the two wedding bands alone were worth over £550 pawn value. This meant that the true value was worth a lot more than that. I could never sell the rings and decided to have them melted down into a couple of large crosses, this seemed the best course of action for the rings, as the children would then have something nice from it. My plan is to present the children with the crosses at Christmas. I also had the diamond ring; this was sentimental too, and worth a lot of money. I made myself a promise many years ago during the separation that if the ring was ever sold the money would only go towards something that would benefit the children. I still have no idea what I will do with the money, so I have decided to wait. The one idea I had, was to buy a car each for my eldest two children, and a private number plate for my youngest son. I thought this was a good idea, as he would have the plate for life, and it would only ever increase in value. I always think what we would have had as a family if we had stayed together, and it is clear we would have had a lot. The money spent on the legal fees with the divorce benefited no one, and the messier a divorce gets, the more fees are created that are only a benefit to the legal advisors. It has been extremely difficult for me to forget what I went through, and I still get upset when I think about it all. I needed to clear my mind of it and set myself free of the torment it causes. You can never turn back time, sadly, but you do have control of what happens in the future. I needed to make sure that I didn't repeat any mistakes I had made in my life, but I mostly needed to make sure that I changed how I thought, as thoughts can be very damaging. Thoughts control your mood, your reactions and general behaviour. I started to train my mind to think positively. I would even write down three positive thoughts a day. I would wake up most days and speak aloud, 'today I will be happy.' It started to work; it's amazing how little changes can have such a positive outcome. I came home each day and instead of sitting around watching TV, I would write or pop out for an evening run. You don't have to run far or complete a huge workout. If you are doing regular training of the mind and body, this is enough to keep the mind and body in a healthy state. My chess has always helped me keep my mind sharp, chess is like life, I guess. We should always stand back and think before we move. Analyse each move available to us and always think what will happen in return if we complete that move. I don't think many are aware just how strong the influence parents have on you as we grow. The influence my mother had on me was a negative one, her anger and quick reactions would influence me. I noticed I started to behave in the same manner as I grew into my teenage years. I was angry a lot and would be prone to quick reactions. I hated that my mum had this influence on me, and I wanted to be free from it all. This is why I have been so committed to change.

My ex-wife would at times say to me, 'oh, you been to your mums have you.' This was due to me coming home frustrated and filled with emotions. I wanted to protect my children from it all and the only way of doing that was for me to change as a man, becoming the best version of myself. It was a constant battle, as I wanted my children to have a relationship with my mum, but it needed to be a healthy one. My mum was prone to slagging me off to my ex-wife and even my children, so it was a tough one. The real difficulty with wanting to change and succeeding in change, is that previous matters stay on your files, and those matters can affect the change you have made. The breaches of orders I committed, although very minor in the whole scheme of things, stay on my file and look far worse than they are. I find it very difficult to forgive my ex-wife for causing these convictions to be on my files. I mean, how on earth can a loving father ignore eleven missed telephone calls from his fourteen-year-old daughter who was desperate for money, and how could a mother allow a police officer to question a child about her loving father who simply messaged his daughter about money. It is wrong that I have certain convictions on my file. It is also annoying to know, that if I was educated to the level I am today, I would have pleaded not guilty to those convictions and would have been extremely confident of being acquitted of all charges. We have no idea how much certain incidents can affect us. We commit what appears to be minor offences when we are young, we commit them without any real concern for our future. It is only when we are older that we begin to realise, sadly. Due to one of my convictions involving a suspended sentence, one of them will stay on my file forever. It is the conviction which involved a breach of a family court order. The details of the conviction are that I responded to my daughter via WhatsApp telling her to be good for her mum, as she is a good mother, and telling her to not worry and that I will transfer her money, also, if ever she needs anything to let me know. This demonsatres how pathetic and dangerous the family court is when it comes to criminalising loving parents. Losing my father was a reality check with how life can be taken from us very quickly. It has encouraged me to do more, so I recently booked a holiday in the spare of the moment with my boys to Crete, which was an amazing experience. There is nothing better than seeing your children happy. I returned home from Crete and just two weeks later, I went on holiday to Portugal with my cousin who is now ex-army. My cousin's friend, Barney, who he served with, joined us. He is probably one of the nicest guys I have ever met. It's been a pleasure in making him a friend. I have never laughed as much as I did on that holiday. It was all thanks to Barney. We laughed so much during a vineyard tour; I had my picture taken with Candy for a laugh. Candy being an American we met who worked at the vineyard, she gave us a tour of the vineyard that afternoon. I needed that holiday so much; it helped me with the grieving process a lot, as I have been struggling a lot recently with the loss of my dad.

Chapter Sixteen

Law

I fell in love with law very quickly during my studies, I love everything about it. I feel very strongly that the family courts need reform, due to this, I no longer have any love or passion for family law. My only interests are in the areas of civil and criminal law. I have many interests in the principles set in landmark cases, *Donoghue v Stevenson* [1932] AC 562 is a perfect example. This case fascinated me, and it was this bit of case law that first ignited my passion in law. I have not been allowed to give advice, as I am not qualified, but I have provided general advice. I have even assisted a few people with completing documents and statements that were needed when wanting to put forward a claim to the court. I assisted my female friend, this was the only female friend I have had since ending my last relationship, November 2021. She was a good friend to me, and I was in return. I successfully assisted her in gaining a judgement for approximately £23,000 plus interest. I do feel that this was the correct outcome, as this is a typical matter that involved a share of a property. The couple were not married, and the young female did not have her name on the mortgage. She had been advised that there was nothing that she could do, and this did appear to be the case, especially if considering the principles set in, *Stack v Dowden* [2007] UKHL 17, but there is so much more to it than that. I feel so many solicitors these days want a matter handed to them on a plate with all evidence available. That is not realistic, and work is involved at times.

I simply approached the matter differently, as I first requested copies of all bank transfers that she had made during the time that the house was originally purchased. I did this, as it may demonstrate an intention. I mean, why on earth would anyone transfer thousands during a time of purchasing a property, and coincidently the person who receives these sums, purchases a property with a good-sized deposit. I put the statement together in a good manner and demonstrated that she expressed an intention to also be part of the purchase of the property. However, I also demonstrated how she was placed under duress in not having her name added to the mortgage. I had evidence, such as bank transfers and nasty text messages to add weight to the claim. I am very aware that I am more than capable of putting forward a case and conducting a good level of advocacy, sadly, the bar course provider has not allowed me to retake the assessments that contained tech issues during the remote setting, and this has forced me to reassess my goals. There are many options open to me in law, and I have recently applied for a few of those options. I have been accepted to complete a second master's degree, and I have also applied to complete my police station qualification. This will all assist me in creating a career in law. I also hope to complete my PHD in the years to come, and that will allow me to one day teach, and maybe write books relating to law. It is important to not ever give up on dreams. Yes, at times we may need to reconsider options and even change direction, but we must never give up on the dream. I have had to change my direction multiple times, and it has caused me to lose some motivation at times, but I always rediscover my motivation due to finding a passion in a new route to my goal. I want my story to help youngsters see that no matter what your goal is, you can always achieve it somehow. The most important part is that you must never give up.

I want the story to create a reminder with what is important and what is a waste of time. The most valuable and precious commodity we have is time, it cannot be replaced. You can always replace money and items, but never time. I get upset when I see wasted talent, and I do believe that I was a wasted talent. I was always capable of achieving academically, but I chose the wrong road every time as a youngster. I chose to waste my time, to mess about, and foolishly thought that it was of no harm getting into trouble or hanging out with the wrong crowd. I look back today, and I get upset when thinking how much time I wasted. I want to shout from the roof tops so that every youngster can hear my story and take note of my advice. There was a time when I was very talented footballer; I was even approached when representing the local territorial army. A scout wanted to come and watch me play for my local team, but the issue with that was, I was not representing any local football team at that time. I was talented in so many areas, but due to my behaviour issues as a youngster my opportunities became limited. Studying law has helped me gain so much self-awareness that was lacking. I began examining every incident I came across, as though I am a judge considering orders. I would often think how my ex-wife refuses at times to co-parent, but I then stand back, and would begin to examine the situation, often concluding that it would not benefit the children for me to hold grudges and instead to continue setting the best example I can set. I would often attend courts to watch trials, to also analyse the different barrister's advocacy styles. The one thing I noticed from all the shadowing I had completed and viewing of trials, was that none of the cases appeared to be anything like the case law I would research whilst studying my degree. The reality is that the exciting case law is rare, and often the cases that a barrister would be working on would be average matters that didn't involve much excitement at all. In 2021 I became friends with a female who had some form of legal training. She owned a business that provided legal advice to defendants who were held at police stations. I would often shadow her whilst she was providing legal advice. I wasn't impressed with her level of legal knowledge, as it appeared limited. She basically made a few notes and recommended that the defendant respond with, 'no comment' as much as possible. The female was attractive and during one late evening whilst she was driving home, she made a pass at me. I was shocked, as I knew that she was in a relationship and this for me was an immediate no, as I would never date anyone who is in a relationship of any kind. The areas I grew up in, such as Hillside Avenue, other areas in Huyton, although extremely rough, still contained many morals that would be instilled in a youngster whilst growing up, not going near another man's woman was one of them. The more I studied law, the more I became frustrated looking back at my own experience, as I knew the few convictions I have against my name should not be there, and if educated to the level I am today, I would have successful had the convictions set aside, and this is the issue with law at times. There are so many people out there who are advised to plead guilty, to receive a 25% discount for the early guilty plea, when in fact, they may have a very good case in proving in part or all their innocence. I was treated so badly and provoked to a sickening level by my ex-wife's solicitor. The situation got that bad, that my legal advisor even drafted a letter to send to their firm and warn them that they would act unless the provoking harassment stopped. I have kept that letter ever since, as it is good evidence to demonstrate that I was very much an innocent man with most of what went on. I was getting texts messages and even calls late of an evening from my ex-wife's solicitor, who would state, 'reply to my email now.' There was no please, or Mr, nothing polite about the approach. It was all very abrupt and almost aggressive. I understand today why he was behaving in this manner, it was simply to create a bigger issue than what there was, as this way it creates more legal fees. I am also aware today that his firm was not doing too well, so it all makes total sense, and why he sued me for hurt feelings. It was all to generate a form of income, and my children would be the victims in the middle of it all. I went through so much that was wrong, I only realised as much once I became legally educated. My ex-wife asked me to transfer near £3,000 for a holiday, when she knew that she had applied for a non-molestation order just weeks before, in turn knowing full well that I would not be able to go on such a holiday, so it was deceiving me. I did threaten to call the police, and her legal advisor was attempting to provide me with legal advice regarding that matter, of which is not allowed due to a conflict of interest. I look back at the incident and I try to see all from my ex-wife's perspective, and I am aware she thought she was only doing what was best for the children. She may have been struggling to pay for the holiday at that time. I am okay with it all now, as my children got to go on holiday, and their happiness is all what matters to me. Keeping the letters that my legal advisor drafted helped me a lot, as it was almost solid evidence showing that it was me being treated badly. The issue that I had was that the family court didn't appear interested in the provoking and wrongful behaviour being committed towards me, they were only interested in my reactions. This is what I dislike about family law, as it is unfair and wrong in many areas. The family courts must be approached in a very particular manner, and unless you have dealt with them before, you would never know this. If anyone has children, for me, you have a duty to put their best interests at the forefront and making matters go to a family court is not putting their best interests at the forefront. I do understand that a lot of matters, sadly, must go before the family court, as it is in the child's best interests, especially if the children are witnessing mental or physical abuse. Adults also need protection at times from harassment, and there are orders, such as a non-molestation that can provide protection. The issue I have is that these orders appear to be handed out with ease at times. There appears to be no test set in passing an order for these protection orders and that for me is wrong, as the orders are very serious and if breached can carry a prison sentence, so I feel a very strict criteria should be met before a non-molestation order is issued. I feel that the court need to take in all evidence, and they do at times, but in my case, they didn't take into consideration the behaviour towards me. I was a litigant in person at the time and was unable to put my case across in a good manner. The other issue with family courts, I feel, is the fact that, as an example, if a woman states that she has suffered physical abuse, with no real evidence, as none is needed in a way, as the burden of proof is lower than that of a criminal court, she may be provided legal aid. The issue I have with this, is that the other party may be a litigant in person, and this creates an unfair balance in the court. The court will end up having an experienced barrister, for instance, against an inexperienced litigant in person. This is not in the best interest of justice.

We see no reason as to why our client should not be spending regular time with the children and we trust that your client recognises and supports the children spending regular time with their Father.

Finally, we feel compelled to raise with you our concerns in respect of the tone and nature of the various correspondence that has been sent to our client in respect of all matters from your Mr. ███████████.

Having considered your company website, we note that it is suggested that Mr. ██████ deals with all matters in a ████████ ██ ██ ██ ███ ████████' We would suggest that the correspondence that we have read and seen is far pleasant and ████ ███ ███ ████.

Our client has provided us with a copy of a text message to which he received from mobile telephone number ████████████ at 20.50pm which read:

'I need a reply to that email now. ████████████.

It is unknown as to whether Mr. ██████ is using his own personal mobile telephone to communicate with our client, yet it is clear that the tone and timing of this text message is wholly inappropriate. We believe that this text message is almost threatening and could be seen as harassment to a litigant in person. Our client was not compelled to respond to any communication that was sent to him, nor was there any legal obligation on him to respond.

If it is the case that your Mr. ██████ is using his personal mobile telephone to contact our client, then we hold concerns in respect of data protection. If this mobile telephone were to be stolen, then our client's details would be in the public domain to which he did not consent to. We trust that you will be aware of the strict guidelines that regulate client confidentiality

Sadly, the text message referred to above was not in isolation as we were horrified to be provided with a further text message which was again sent from the same telephone which read:

'Whether you go to the police or not is your choice I cannot control that.

I would however point out that whilst you are given permission to talk to the kids about non adult matters you are not to use this as an opportunity to badger my client about money

I will be advising my client that if the conversation strays on to adult matters, she should end the call

I doubt very much the police will be interested in your complaint and I would suggest that it would be better for you not to pursue that matter at this time.'

Another page from the letter my legal advisor drafted.

Not only is your Mr. ▮▮▮ making a direct insult to our client at the suggestion that he would utilise the opportunity of speaking to his children to *'badger'* your client, but we also trust that you will note that within this message, your Mr. ▮▮▮ is offering advice to our client. This places Mr. ▮▮▮ in conflict when representing Mrs. ▮▮▮. Mr ▮▮▮ will know he cannot advise both parties in a single matter.

In addition to the wholly inappropriate text message communication that has been sent to our client we have considered all of the emails that have been sent to our client direct and nearly all emails are written in a tone which is inflammatory, contain remarks which are derogatory and show a distinct lack of respect for a litigant in person. For example, none of the emails are addressed to either 'Mr ▮▮▮ / Dear ▮▮▮ and we would suggest that if Mr ▮▮▮ had instructed solicitors, then such correspondence would not have been sent in the tone and manner that it has.

A number of emails contain errors to which it appears have been used as indirect threats towards our client. We note that in one email sent direct to our client, it has been suggested that if our client were to attend the children's school then he would be duly arrested for breaching the Non-Molestation Order that is in existence. Having considered the terms of the Non-Molestation Order there is no clause that would prevent our client from attending the children's school. This is something that we would reasonably expect your Mr. ▮▮▮ to be aware of. We are concerned that the threat of our client being arrested was used to simply deter our client from attending the children's school.

The communications that our client has received have caused him a significant amount of unnecessary stress and anxiety due to their nature and tone.

In such circumstances we can confirm that we have advised our client to contact the Solicitors Regulation Authority to report his concerns in respect of the conduct of your ▮▮▮

We trust you will be aware of the recent Tribunal decision in the matter of the *Solicitors Regulation Authority v Lucatello*, where Mr. Lucatello was subsequently fined for making derogatory remarks / sending inappropriate communications to a litigant in person.

It is with grave concern that it appears that your ▮▮▮ has developed a personal interest in this matter. We note from an email that was sent on the ▮▮▮ ▮▮▮ direct to our client, that it was indicated that your client was not agreeable to our client spending time with the children whatsoever. This email was sent the day after our respective clients had agreed between themselves for our client to spend time with the children. This causes our client to questions as to whether your Mr. ▮▮▮ is ascertaining his client's instructions prior to sending communication.

It is likely that our respective client's relationship will never resolve itself, yet our respective clients will always maintain a relationship with one and other, albeit a one of separated parents. There will become a time where our respective client's will need to agree matters between themselves, without the assistance of

The family courts, like all courts, are extremely busy. I have shadowed Judges, and I am aware that they have a tough job to do, and I do know that they do the best that they can do. I don't want my chapter on law to appear that I am against the courts or dislike Judges, as it couldn't be further from the truth. I have the upmost respect for judges and the court. I am aware it is difficult; we view it as unfair at times. We know all the details of our own background and case facts, but the judge doesn't know you personally and can only go off first impression and the details put before them. I didn't paint a good picture of myself when I first entered the family court, as I was defensive, because I thought I was the victim in many areas. I couldn't afford a legal adviser at the start of the process, and I struggled to know what the best approach was. I feel that if a parent is not abusive in any way, to others or themselves, not bad mouthing the other parent to the children, and if they are a caring, loving and a providing parent, then, there should never be a reason for that parent to be kept from the children. Sadly, this is not the case a lot of the time. The reason I have added copies of the drafted letter my legal advisor wrote, is to highlight that not all legal professionals behave in a professional manner. It is of importance to be aware of this, and important to not react during provoking confrontations. We all react, and it is difficult not to during an emotional process. I noticed that the odd Judge didn't appear to like litigants, mostly due to the fact they are not legally trained, and it can take more of the courts time, but these types of Judges need to be aware that litigants deserve a level of respect.

'It has often been viewed that litigants in person are a nuisance to the court, when in fact the court is a nuisance to the litigant, speaking a foreign language during an emotional process.'

'All too often the litigant in person is regarded as a problem for judges and for the court system rather than a person for whom the system of civil justice exists.'

Lord Woolf, Access to justice, interim Report June 1995

Some judges do forget at times that the system is there for the litigant and should not be treated differently because they are a litigant. At the first hearing, the family judge asked me why I didn't have a legal adviser and when I told her she puffed and blowed when I stated I couldn't afford one at that time. These are the areas of family law that I dislike, especially with how, at times, Cafcass appear to mark down a parent due to how they react. When not seemingly considering the stress and upset a parent would be experiencing during the emotional family court process. I feel that there is no difference at all with asking a person to not react to a burning flame being held under their hand, asking them, to not cry in pain or even flinch. There is no difference to what one suffers internally to externally, and in fact, internal and emotional damage can be a lot more severe at times. If a loving father or mother are told that they cannot see their children, it won't go down to well, especially if that parent is of no harm to the children in any way. Try stealing a newborn cub from a lion, you will not get a good response. So many forget that we are all animals, yet they want us to act like robots, robots who have no feelings and never react. It just isn't realistic, and that is what upsets me about the family court process. The government have promised for many years now that they will reform the family court system, and it is now long overdue. I would like to finish of this chapter, by highlighting that I do feel that the criminal justice system is fair most of the time. The prosecution has the burden of proving all elements of the offence. I feel far too many plead guilty at speed, when in fact, they may be guilty only in part, or at times, innocent. They become fearful, occasionally, this due to incorrect legal advice. Some legal advisors seem to like a straight forward in and out of court situation. I have been accused by police officers of using my mobile phone twice in the past three years. I pleaded not guilty and won both cases. The evidence they produced, was just their statements. The last case at a Liverpool court turned out to be a funny one. I was accused of using my mobile phone whilst driving on the M62 towards Liverpool. The officer turned up at my home, at Lymm, Cheshire. This is many miles from Liverpool. He turned up aggressive, accusing me of using my mobile phone. I asked the two officers to leave, but a few months later, I received documents in the post. I pleaded not guilty and attended a trail. The incident happened in 2023, so by this time I was well trained in law, especially in all areas of advocacy. I cross examined the officer, asking him what colour my mobile phone was, he didn't know, but stated he was 100% certain I had a mobile phone. I had presented some doubt with regards to the description of the phone. I went on to ask the officer if my window was up or down, he couldn't remember. At this stage, I asked the court if I may put forward an application for, *'no case to answer'*, using *Galbraith*. The matter of *R v Galbraith* [1981] 1 WLR 1039, set out the test for the court to consider when hearing an application for, *'no case to answer.'* The officer became angry and even shouted in court, so my advocacy skills were clearly of a good standard. My, *'no case to answer'* application was refused. I was then to be cross examined, but the prosecutor was weak, I feel. She didn't apply any form of pressure at all. She allowed me to divert and move away from certain subjects, were as when I cross examined. I kept the officer in my lane and having him answer only to the questions I put to him. The officer had stated he saw a charger lead and I was asked about this. I responded stating that it was not a charger lead, but string hanging from my rear-view mirror. The string was there, as when I collected my young son from him mothers, his cat, *Mylo*, would enter my car and play with the string as I waited outside for my son. I then produced a large picture of *Mylo* in my car. The Magistrates looked at the picture and immediately voiced a, 'ah, isn't he a lovely cat.' I had to stay composed, as I was ready to burst out laughing, due to the magistrates all looking at the picture of the cat, and all seemingly voicing, 'ah'. I was acquitted of all charges and free to go. The prosecution afterwards congratulated me and wished me luck with the rest of my studies.

Mylo the cat in my car

Chapter Seventeen

Christmas

Christmas has always been my favourite time of year. I feel that is due to the happy memories I have as a child when visiting my grandmothers at Christmas. I can still remember walking up to my grandmothers when we lived at Bruton Road, I must have been around age six at the time. I remember the snow and even remember the excitement I felt the closer we got to my grandmother's house. I remember a lot from Bruton Road, and even remember getting a large truck one year that was remote controlled. Me and my dad were playing with it in the kitchen area, I think that this was also the year I got an electric piano. These are good memories that I have. The bad memories started once we moved from Bruton Road to Gentwood Road. Each year, one of my uncles would dress as Santa and hand out presents, this was an idea that my grandmother created. My grandmother was always amazing with her grandchildren, she made Christmas special for us all. It was my uncles' dressing up as Santa that gave me the idea of also pretending to be Santa each Christmas eve for my own children. I would climb onto the roof and put on the voice of Santa. My children would smile and laugh with excitement. I would return at the front door pretending that I had been to the local shop. My children would run with excitement to tell me that I had missed Santa. I still often look back at the videos and it brings a tear to my eye, as I wish that my children were still at that age. I miss dressing up as Santa, but who knows, the Santa suit may be put on again one day.

Christmas is that one time of the year where we all come together as a family and as a community. I do feel that we are losing the Christmas spirit little by little each year. It is being taken from us, which is extremely sad, as we are a Christian country who have a long history of Christmas traditions. Christmas for me, since my divorce, has never been the same. It has lost its spark and most of its excitement. Christmas is about watching your children open presents; it is about watching your children smile at the decorations, and for all the family admiring a Christmas tree, a Christmas tree that is always far too large for the house that it's in. I still put up as many Christmas decorations as possible, and even buy the largest tree I can find, but most of the Christmas period I am alone. I will buy far too much Christmas food and stock up on wine as though I am expecting a large family to visit. I will sit there of an evening and imagine that my children are all at home playing board games. I picture that their mother is laughing at them cheating and that I am asking to join in. I then picture us all getting ready for a Christmas movie on the sofa. Christmas can always bring on some anxiety, as it is leading towards New Years Eve. My memory or body seem to remember the shooting from time to time, and it brings on a tense feeling. I also seem to get upset as I look back when thinking about the trauma I experienced. I always try to think of happy thoughts, even of the times when my sister and I opened presents each year. My parents would always wait for the main present to be opened an hour after we opened all the rest. They would make us think that was all we got, and as we began playing with the presents, my parents would pretend that there was a knock on the door and Santa had forgotten two more presents. Each year, it would always be either a bike or a snooker table for me, and my sister would always have a large dolls house for her Barbies.

During the Christmas week, I would sit on my sofa looking at the clock, watching each evening pass at speed. I would sit thinking that I need to get more food in, as though the shops are due to close for a month. I would always be quickly reminded that I am on my own and no one is visiting. Despite this loneliness feeling, I still wouldn't jump into a relationship for the sake of being with someone. I would much rather be alone and lonely than be with the wrong person. I am aware that I need to one day meet someone, and I say the word, *need*, due to the amount I have to offer. I have so much love and loyalty to offer, that it would be a great shame for it to go to waste. I am suited to a relationship and hope to one day meet the love of my life, and who knows, I may one day have another child and get to climb on to the roof as Santa once more.

Christmas at Gentwood Road (me and my sister).

I did spend Christmas with a couple of girlfriends after my divorce, but it was nothing compared to when spending Christmas with my children or as a family. I decided to buy a dog one year, as I thought it would be a great way for me to not feel so lonely. I also knew that my boys would love the idea of having a dog. I have always loved the Belgian Malinois breed, but it is far from a family pet. It is a working dog and constantly full of energy, they can get bored at speed and need walking daily. My eldest son fell immediately in love with the dog and grew an attachment to him. I knew getting the dog was a bad decision by me, and even my ex-wife commented saying that the breed wasn't the best idea, and she was right. My eldest son was due to start college at the time and I was due to start my next stage of studying, which involved many visits to London. I named the dog, Sabre, this was because this was the same name given to the dogs my father had. We had two German Shepherds, and they were both named, Sabre. I got Sabre at the worst time possible, he grew fast, and even though he was easy to train, he was becoming a handful. I contacted the breeder with the aim of handing him back, but my eldest son was not impressed, and I could tell he was upset with it all, but it was cruel to keep a dog that we couldn't give him what he needed. Me and my son visited the breeder the day we were handing him back. We were told that a new owner was lined up, who owned a large garden. My son was happy at the idea knowing that Sabre would be better suited to a large garden, but this fell through, and within two days another hopeful owner came forward who agreed to take on the dog. The day we walked away from Sabre I will never forget, Not because of the dog as much, but mostly because I knew I upset my son. My son today doesn't even like talking about Sabre, as it causes him upset, so I always try to avoid the topic of Sabre.

Christmas at my parents didn't resemble what Christmas was like at my Grandparents. My father would always say he was tired, and want an afternoon's sleep on the sofa, and my mother would drink wine to the point that she also needed a sleep. My parents didn't seem excited for Christmas, and one year even stated that they didn't want to have a Christmas tree, as it was too much fuss. This annoyed me, as Christmas wasn't about them and their wants, it is about the children and grandchildren. I started to visit my parents less and less, as I would always come away upset. I first came up with the idea of cooking a Christmas dinner on Boxing Day when I was married. We invited the in-laws over, who are the nicest people you could wish to meet. The first year didn't go well, as the neighbour at the rear was building a ground floor extension and had the cheek to ask me for some of my land so that the extension would not be on an angle. I refused, but on Boxing Day they still went ahead and deliberately pulled down the fence. I immediately went round on Boxing Day and had a huge confrontation with the neighbour, who was drunk at the time. They attempted to put the fence line back in a different location and a location to suit their build. I got solicitors involved and we settled out of court, but I only got what the fence cost. I got no damages or compensation, but a week later the builders continued with their terrible attitude, leaving boards in my garden, without warnings. One evening a board flew in the wind and hit me, so I made a claim for personal injury and was awarded £6,500. Some may say I was wrong making a claim, but these builders had no permission to enter my garden. They didn't just enter my garden, they started to use my rear garden as a storage area. My two young children couldn't play out in the garden for a six-month period.

The following Boxing day involved no one visiting, as I was on my own this year due to my ex-wife leaving. It was a very sad year, but thankfully the following year my parents agreed to visit Boxing Say with my brother and his family. We made it a regular theme, and my boys appeared to get excited for the day. I am so glad this Boxing Day meal was introduced, as it has allowed me to have good memories of my dad during the Christmas period. Christmas today involves just me and my boys. It gets very upsetting for me, as I miss my father and my family being around. I am aware I have highlighted abuse I suffered and even stated that Christmas was not as good as when we visited my grandparents, but that doesn't mean to say I am not thankful for the presents my parents worked hard for. My parents tried their best to make Christmas as happy as possible and for many years they succeeded.

Christmas will now always be that time of year I reflect on my childhood, and I try to remember the good times with my dad. My father was the one who always tried to bring the family together, he was a good grandfather who loved all his grandchildren equally. I am sure my nephew, nieces and my own children are all aware of that. I hope that they too have fond memories of my dad. My dad wanted to take us for a family drink at times, and me and my sister did join him a few times, but that faded out, sadly. I visit my sister's home Christmas Day now, and the first time this happened was an amazing experience. They are both lovely people with a perfect family. My nephew is the youngest and a giant for his age. He resembles me at that age, with his big bushy blond curly hair. My nieces are all brilliant, and each of them have a different personality. Family was very important to my dad, and it was always a battle with my mum when it came to keeping the family together, as my mum always appeared to want conflict, whereas my dad would want the family together, most of the time, and all getting on. I suggested to my sister for her to bring her youngest around Christmas eve, so that I could get on the roof as Santa once more, but it has not happened yet. I even suggested it to the female friend I had, it's as though I am yearning to experience the family life once more. If I would have stayed married, we would have had five children by now, and this doesn't mean to say that I don't want any more children. I would relish the chance of falling in love and having more children, but sadly it doesn't appear to be happening for me. Families should not have to wait for Christmas to spend time with each other, we all should have occasions weekly. My grandparent's home would have an event every Sunday, and it was such a lovely time where the family were together. My aunties would try to help my grandmother cook the Sunday dinner, and that would be a challenge, as my grandmother would dislike anyone helping her at times. I tried to make Sunday special, and started to cook a Sunday dinner, but it didn't take with my two boys. It is so hard when you are alone, as it takes a family to be a family sometimes. When one parent struggles in gaining the children's attentions, the other parent steps in with their own approach, and parents without thinking are working as a team, using tactics that seem to work in most families. It worked in my family; my approach was different to that of my ex-wife's. My children's mother is very good at getting the children together and having them find an interest in what she sets up. She was always good at that, no matter what idea she came up with, it was always a good idea and the children, and I would always be excited with it all. If my ex-wife stated that there would be a Sunday dinner, the children would show an interest, whereas my approach seems to have less appeal.

We all act as though we have all the time in the world, sadly, it's far from it, as time passes at speed. I always try to have holidays spare at Christmas week. I create a whole movie list that always involves: Christmas vacation, Polar Express, Home Alone, The Snowman, It's a Wonderful Life (My sisters and my own favourite movie), The Bishops Wife, and much more. One year I put on Die Hard, and it was the first time my eldest son had watched it. He ran to his youngest brother making him aware how brilliant the movie was. I still class it as a Christmas movie, although some will disagree. I often think about taking my boys away at Christmas, but it would remove the family home spirit. I miss looking outside watching my boys play with their new toys, and annoyingly these days, many children are in fear when playing out due to the idiots who speed around the built-up areas, or the pathetic signs stating, 'no ball games.' What has happened to the world, there's no kid friendly streets anymore. People are constantly moaning about children playing, but they are the first ones to also complain when kids get up to no good when bored. I watch my sons' open their presents each year, and I compare it to how I was, and it is different, I just feel the magic of Christmas has gone slightly. I am aware that the country has gone through a change, and there are many who now seem to hate the name, 'Christmas.' They want it to be called, 'The Holidays.' I know what I say to that, and it is most definitely a swear word. The world can't see that the changes they are making is not for the better, it is for the worse. I hope they leave Christmas alone and I pray that the magic of how Christmas once was returns.

Chapter Eighteen

Perceptive

I do feel I have a good ability to be perceptive, as I am very good at standing back and looking at all viewpoints. This is lacking in the world today, sadly. So many of us convince ourselves that our viewpoint is correct, and we decide this without looking at other people's viewpoints. I have highlighted how I was badly treated a few times, but when I view matters from my ex-wife's viewpoint, I realise that she was only doing what she thought was right, she was also taking advice from her legal adviser, although it was terrible advice, she wasn't to know that. Don't get me wrong, there are many areas where I feel my ex-wife is very wrong, but that is irrelevant today. We must all view matters from different standpoints, and yes, that is easy to say, as we are all human and emotions can get the better of us, especially if someone has done us wrong. If we have children, we must always be aware that the children may view matters very differently. I didn't take this into consideration when I found out about my ex-wife's affair, and instead, in front of the children, they heard me on the phone calling their mum bad names. I also told the children that their mum had cheated on me. I would tell myself, that because I have not threatened anyone, smashed anything up, or hit anyone, then it was okay. The fact is emotional damage can be worse at times. So many of us when finding out about an affair become emotional and almost aggressive, which is sad really, as we only do ourselves more damage. The correct course of action would be to stand back and analyse the matter in full detail. Ask yourself, 'what and who caused this?' as it may just be yourself. I also feel that we all should ask ourselves, 'do we even love this person?' So many are in false relationships. A relationship they started as they can't handle being alone, or they entered it due to the benefits that the other person provides. So many are in relationships for all kinds of reasons, and a lot of the time, love isn't one of them. One could state that cheating occurs due to the person not loving their partner, otherwise why would they cheat you may ask, but I also feel that cheating is a sign of immaturity. I do believe that many cheat as they are too immature to handle a real relationship that may even have a real future. They can't handle the boring parts, or the parts where there isn't any spark. It is like a child sitting in front of a blank TV screen, it would be a matter of minutes before they went looking for something else to occupy their minds. All relationships have blank screen periods, and at times it can occur regularly. If you are mature, you would realise by instantly running elsewhere for some excitement, you will only find that it is temporary, as most affairs are, sadly. You then return to see your stable life that you once had, is now gone. People just don't look at the risks involved, or even look at what is at stake. If I offered you a full year with the most attractive person in exchange for twenty years of your childhood and family memories, would you take it? I would hope not, as memories is all we have. When a married person with children cheats, they don't just ruin the marriage, they ruin all that comes with it. The millions of memories, the board games, the arguments over tea, the holidays, or weekends away, Christmas movies whilst you are all on the sofa fighting for space. The list is endless, and the sad part is, we don't take any of that into consideration when running off for a bit of fun. I am aware of a few friends who have cheated on their wives. They all end up in the same position, the affair never lasts or doesn't turn out like advertised. The children lose out mostly, as they end up seeing one parent less than the other, and to see less of dad or mum will have a negative impact on any child. A few of my friends, after they split, they end up single and struggling. I believe cheats end up with cheats, as both parties will be aware one or both is cheating, and if you are okay with that, then you have a few issues in my book. I would never go near anyone who is in a relationship, if you try to build a house on precarious ground, you will always live with the fear of the house falling at any moment. If you start a relationship with someone who cheated, surely you would always live with the fear of them cheating again. I have cheated and many times, but only when I was a teenager, I would never cheat on anyone today and have not for many years. I am now a man, and a real man is aware what's at stake if cheating. So many never mature, or at times, as I believe, it is just in their nature to cheat or be a bad person. It's like the movie, Charlie and the Chocolate Factory, some eggs are just bad. I carry one little story with me in my mind, and it has helped me on many occasions when trying to understand people who have done me wrong.

'One day a frog was taking a walk along the riverside, when suddenly, he notices a scorpion. The scorpion approaches the frog, and the frog instantly becomes vigilant. The scorpion asks the frog for a lift across the river, but the frog replies, 'no, because you would surly sting me Mr Scorpion.' The scorpion assures the frog that he will not sting him and begs for a lift across the river. The scorpion is very convincing and eventually the frog believes the scorpion and trusts that he will not sting him. The scorpion jumps on the frogs back and they began their journey across the river, but halfway across the frog feels a burning sensation in his neck and

realises that the scorpion had stung him. The frog began to drown and as they both sank, the frog cries out, 'why Mr scorpion, why did you sting me, as now both of us will surely drown.' The scorpion replies, 'I am sorry Mr frog, I can't help it. It's in my nature.'

Humans are like this too; it is just in some people's nature to sting others. The issue with these people is that they are so very convincing to begin with and people are easy to grow trust with these people. I am not saying for one minute I have been innocent all my life, as I have not. It was only when first meeting my ex-wife that I changed in so many ways. The moment she became pregnant I instantly became a man. The moment I held my daughter was the greatest day of my life, and right there and then I promised her that I will be a good father and a good man. It was just very sad that during that time I was very unwell with my PTSD, something that I tried to hide from the outside world.

When I was promoted to regional manager whilst working in Irish transport, it was a role that carried much responsibility, as I would manage many staff. I would always have to look at matters from the workers perspective. It was the job role that enabled me to grow as a man and start to look at matters differently. The same happened when I started studying law, I started to perfect an ability of looking at matters from all angles. This is an important skill to possess, as it allows you to see were, at times, you may be in the wrong. To fix any problem, you first need to find out what it is. The one issue I have always come across in my life, is that people will always judge you from one negative experience that they have had with you. People don't seem to give others a second chance. I started to behave at school towards the end, but the teachers didn't trust that I may have changed, and instead treated me like I was behaving bad, even when I was well behaved. People are like this as adults too, if you have a run in with your neighbour over a parking space, they will always hold a grudge against you, without ever viewing matters from your view point. I have had so many run-ins with the neighbours where I live. The neighbours at the rear of the property smashed up my fence and attempted to steal land, but when I defended my property, other neighbours didn't view it like that. They just saw a young male shouting, and they instantly made up their mind that I was the aggressive one. The one thing that annoyed me is, if that were them, they would probably respond much worse than myself. I have even had cars block my driveway and when I ask people to move it, they turn on you, as if it is you who is in the wrong. I once had a neighbour standing at the front of my driveway talking about me and my family with other neighbours. She was saying that she didn't think my home was broken into when it was. She was introduced to karma that month, as a few weeks passed by and that very neighbour was also broken into. These people go to church too, there are so many fake people about these days. They pretend to be someone they are not, when the truth is, they are nothing but nasty bullies. I have a property in Lymm / Cheshire, but I am currently considering a whole new start in the south. I have been viewing properties in Bristol of late, as it would benefit my want for a career in law if being based there. I just need to take into consideration what benefits my children. I could always get my youngest at weekends, and he would benefit from the change of surroundings, I guess. It would do him good. I must also think about my eldest son, but I have a good amount of equity and could always buy a small property in Cheshire where he could live. I have many options, and that is all thanks to me fighting in court to save the home during the divorce process, as today, it has a good amount of equity in it. Being part of the local Cheshire churches is one thing that I have tried to do many times but failed.

I have not failed due to my want, but failed due to how churches can be stuck up. I attended a local church, and I was approached by the vicar who said, 'You are young, you may be better off going a different church as they are all old fogey's here.' What that vicar didn't realise was, who takes over that generation and we wonder why so many churches are closing due to people not visiting. They don't visit, as a lot of churches have this stuck-up attitude. I even visited another local church in the area where I live. I visited the vicar's home, and we discussed Christianity. I was asked how I felt about forgiveness, and I replied with a very honest opinion, I stated that I personally struggle that God may forgive people who have hurt children. The vicar's wife became aggressive and with a tone she cut me off with, 'so you think you know better than God, do you?' I know now why my father lost his faith due to these people who feel that are religiously superior to others. My father attended this church but had a few bad experiences and lost his faith. I still prayed at my father's hospital bedside the day he passed. I asked God to accept him into heaven and to forgive his sins. I wish I could turn back time and have the abilities I have today. I would have avoided so many issues in my life. It is hard when one has been mentally unwell, and that is another matter that people do not consider today. They see someone behaving badly, but don't ever think why. If someone was bleeding, people instantly rush to the persons aid, but if they can't see the injury, they become less likely to help, especially if it is a mental injury. I don't for one minute support any form of violence, it would be correct for people to avoid violence. I once witnessed a girl crying, and what upset me was, every person who passed her, looked at her and looked away. I walked over and asked her if she needed any help, she explained that she was upset due to separating from her boyfriend. This may appear a minor issue, but what if it wasn't, what if she had just been attacked in some way. You would be shocked if you knew how many attacks happen in broad daylight, even sex attacks. The world today is not a nice place, and I feel that is because people have become selfish, or people only look at matters only from their own viewpoint. I have approached schools with the idea of giving talks about my experience and how an academic environment saved me.

Not one school have replied, as a lot do judge you from a minor civil matter on my DBS, of which may be discrimination, as stated. I have a positive message, and I can also understand why kids behave badly. I know what can trigger a positive response, as I have been that badly behaved child. I have achieved a lot academically and in a workplace. I want to tell my story and make badly behaved kids aware how important time is. I want to make as many aware as possible, that if I can achieve academically, then anyone can. We live in a world where everyone instantly judges others, and what chance do any of us have if the likes of schools and many workplaces instantly judge us, and without even seeing you. People deserve a second chance; they deserve a chance to explain their situation and why they may have certain matters on their DBS file. Schools and many other organisations also need to be educated what is minor and what is serious when it comes to DBS checks, because so many see a few matters and without understanding what the matters are they instantly turn you away. The situation ends up with having a person who has worked so hard to prove themselves, and it all ends up being for nothing. They are discriminating without a second thought. I speak so much about viewing matters from a different viewpoint, to try and understand matters before concluding. The people who need this skill more than anyone else, is a lot schools, workplaces and organisations. The real test for me has been when I did change and become a better man. The moment

I got over my PTSD, this is when the real challenges started. This is when I noticed I was judged for previous minor mistakes. I have tendences to have trust in the system at times and have too much trust in people. I foolishly think that all people are good, or that certain people when representing organisations must be good due to who they represent. It then becomes a huge shock when I come to realise that it doesn't matter who people represent, they can still behave poorly. As an example, the amount of police in the media of late who have committed terrible crimes appears to be on the rise. I still feel it of importance to have a positive outlook. If someone reacts badly or behaves badly towards you, don't jump to assume they are bad, first analyse why the incident happened, as there may be good reasons sometimes. I try to remind my children that the world is bad, but only so that they are on guard. I am aware that I need to remind them and maybe more so that there are good people in this world, and that they should trust others. I don't know, it is so hard at times being a parent. I am lucky and so too is my ex-wife, as we have three perfect children. I only wish that we separated five years after we did, as we would have had another two children within those extra years together. Children are a blessing and nothing other, they should never be ignored, and you should always realise how lucky you are to have them there.

Chapter Nineteen

Goals and Football

I always view goals like getting on an aeroplane and heading to a destination. You set a goal for one destination, you eventually get there and enjoy the holiday. Once you return home, you set another goal for another destination. Most of the time the destinations improve, but If you never set a goal, then you are just flying around in circles going nowhere. You will also one day simply run out of fuel, then you can't go anywhere. I look at the fuel as one's physical ability. So many people decide on their goal far too late. It can be annoying to achieve a goal later in life, as you the realise that you were always capable of it, like me with my academic achievements. I always thought it was impossible for me to gain a degree, when in fact, it was easy overall. Studying for my degree was extremely enjoyable, and this was a surprise, as I always pictured it being boring. It is okay to divert your goals once a while, and we shouldn't beat ourselves up about this. I have failed three parts of the bar course, and I feel that it was at no fault to myself, as there were many tech issues with the software that played a huge part in the remote assessments process. I can sit around crying about it, or I can simply divert and create new goals. I have decided to start a second master's degree, with the aim of completing my PHD. I will do this, and nothing will stand in my way. I am no longer a fan of some universities, as it is clear, for me, that they are money hungry and not too concerned about what the students get in return at times. I am sure there are good universities out there, but the pointless degrees many offer, are a good example how they are going to extremes to make money. Students will get into student debt to complete some degrees that they will not be able to do anything with. Don't get me wrong here, studying is extremely important and there are many benefits to completing a good degree. I highly recommended completing a degree, as it is very enjoyable. I am just highlighting that you shouldn't be surprised if you come across a lack of support from a university and don't be surprised if their complaints procedure is of a terrible standard. Universities need some form of ombudsman to overlook how they conduct business, and hopefully this all improves one day soon. There are many days that pass where I sit and wonder where it all went wrong. I look back at myself driving an expensive car and managing people, but today, I am struggling at times. I often conclude that the divorce caused it all, as the divorce cost over £94,000, this annoys me, even today. There are many reasons why I get annoyed, as an example, If I had used that money to instead make over payments on my mortgage each month. I would not be struggling as much. Most importantly, the children would have benefited. I constantly remind myself at the same time how fortunate I am. I own nice items, such as a £6,000 watch, many collectable items in the home and the home itself. I have a lot more than many, so I shouldn't complain. I never try to call the home, my home, as it isn't mine. This is what my ex-wife didn't realise during the divorce process. The home is a home first, and secondly it is an inheritance, or a providing tool. It is the only inheritance my children have, and I was never going to allow my children to have that taken away from them by some vile legal adviser. A legal adviser who laughed out loud in my face when stating that he will have me evicted from my home and force sell it, leaving me with just a small amount left over, due to him massively under valuing the home with my ex-wife. Thankfully, the court allowed none of it, and I won that matter, but the stress I experienced in later matters when a court did decide that the home will be forcibly sold was terrible. I would cry each evening with worry about losing everything and my children not able to sleep over, as I won't have any home for them to come and stay. This home is the only real home they have ever known. I was so nervous when representing myself at the appeal court. The higher courts are a lot more daunting, and I was overjoyed to have won and have the judgements all set aside. The house was saved once more and my children's future that bit more secure. I will never get over how my ex-wife and her legal adviser valued the house approximately £130,000 below market value. They were only stealing from the children's inheritance and nothing other. I try to make sense of it all and look at matters from all angles, but even then, I struggle to except previous behaviours at times. We all must move on from our past, as we simply don't have the time to waste. I have stated this a few times and I will repeat it again, I am sure my ex-wife was only doing what she thought was best for her and the children, but completely unaware that she was gaining terrible legal advice at the same time, which benefited only her legal advisor. I wonder what is next for me and often wonder where I will end up, and who with. I am aware I analyse myself far too much at times and need to do it less. Right now, I am healthy and getting my fitness back to where it needs to be. I eat healthy and hardly drink alcohol these days. I often test my will power, and recently decided to go sixty-two days without a single drop of alcohol. I also only ever eat Sourdough bread. I don't have milk and avoid sugar. I am looking after me and that is nothing but a good thing. I have faith, not just with my religious beliefs, but also belief in the words my father and what my grandmother spoke.

'If you are doing all the right things in life, then the right things will come to you. It is boring saving money, boring staying in at weekends, boring avoiding alcohol, and boring only ever eating healthy foods. It is exciting getting drunk at times, and it feels good eating fast food, it is also exciting staying up until the early hours at weekends, but what is good for your health and mind and what is bad for it? If you do all the good things for your body and mind, then you will only ever attract good to you, good health, a good career, and good people.'

My dad made this statement to me, and my grandmother stated something very similar. My dad probably voiced it on the way to the fruit market one morning, as that was often when he came out with a life speech. Looking back, he was always right when it came to life advice. I personally feel that we attract what and who we are. If we are a bad person, then we will attract bad people to us, if we are a cheat, then cheats seem to attract cheats. I hope that my belief is true, as I am confident that I am a good man and if I can attract what and who I am today, I will be happy with that. My father gave out great life advice, as stated, but he was terrible when it came to business advice, but life advice, he was the master.

'We all end up with what and who we deserve. We end up with what we deserve from how hard we work, and we end up with who we deserve by who we are as a person. If you are bad, then good people will not stick around for long.'

This is probably my personal favourite, as it makes total sense. This is why I try to work hard and want to keep becoming a better man each day. I am constantly wanting to improve on who I was yesterday. I have a part time job right now, and that means I am working. I am a working man and that gains some respect. I was signed off work for twelve months due to depression and anxiety brought on from the loss of my father and a terrible experience at my previous workplace, but I have decided to work instead of being off sick. I would be better off by £150 per month by being off work sick, but I will lose some self-respect by doing nothing, plus I have a belief that it is healthy to work and keep on the move as much as possible. I do apply for better roles often, but I am now aware that my age may now play a part. I didn't think that day would ever come, but it is here and here at speed. My focus right now is to keep working and head towards my second masters. I am considering doing my second master part-time, but the issue with that is that it will take two years, opposed to one year, and my age is catching up with me, so I need to see what I can afford. Ideally, I want to complete the master's over one year, it just then means that the total payment is then due over one year. The very moment I reached the previous sentence when writing this book, I decided to email the university and make them aware I want to complete my second master's over one year. I will stress about how I will pay it at a later stage. We can always replace money; it is time that we cannot replace. I recently, and for the first time in my life joined a dating site. It is not for me; I hate how you must start a whole new conversation every few moments. I also dislike that the people who you may be talking to, may be talking to other people at the same time. This seems morally wrong to me, I guess I am just very old-fashioned when it comes to dating. Maybe this is the new way now, it is okay to talk to a few at once, but I still find that wrong, as it sets a theme that it is okay to talk to others. It is also obvious that many will keep reserves waiting just in case the relationship doesn't work out. This is my outlook on dating sites, and no one will change my mind either. You may now ask, why on earth am I on a dating site then? It is boredom and nothing other.

I am just bored, as I am on my own constantly these days. I hardly go out, other than to go out for a run and bit of cardio or go to work. I am planning to go out socialising more, as it would be healthy to do so. I coached two young children at chess recently, and I enjoyed that very much. The kids were great, and it was a pleasure offering them advice. I have applied for my master's at speed and for the reason being, I will then feel I am heading towards something. I am aware time is not on my side with my age, and I know me, and I am aware that for me to perform at my best, I must have a few goals in place, and I must be actively working towards those goals. If I have nothing in place I have noticed that I become depressed and start to feel very negative about myself. I have learnt that I am capable of so much, and I don't want that to go to waste. It is important for us to all know what our true abilities are, and once we realise that we are capable of more. It would be a crime to not want to achieve more. I am constantly getting at my sons to achieve and to want to achieve. My eldest son just walks past me now, as he is fed up with the reminders. He makes me laugh, as it is obvious that he is wanting to give the impression he is listening when in fact, he isn't. My home is decorated to a good standard and my son's room is to a standard that makes him happy. It is important to have a clean and tidy environment, as I believe that will create a tidy mind set. A senior American naval officer once said that if you want change, then start with making your bed in the morning. He is exactly right, being tidy and organised from the moment you wake up creates a good mindset. I don't want to feel I am missing out on life by being at home and only working on my goals, so recently I have set a few extra goals, such as getting a power boat for next summer. This will allow me to take my boys away each weekend for water sports.

I have also started to book little trips away, and recently planned another holiday with my sons to Croatia, I must be aware of what I can offer as a man too. It is important we all realise and take note of what we can offer others. I have two young cousins in care, and I want to offer them support as and when I can. Eating healthy and regular exercise creates a positive mindset. I am drinking less alcohol which has had a positive effect on me, and I am now waking up with much more energy. I feel more alert, and my chess appears to be improving too. Everything is heading in the right direction when it comes to my new diet and fitness plan. I just feel I need a woman in my life, and it isn't because I want someone there for the sake of having someone there. I am just very aware that I am a loving and caring man with a lot to offer. I am romantic, giving, and loyal, and I feel that should not all go to waste. I have stated before that we must be aware of what we have to offer, and not allow that to go to waste. This applies to relationships too, I am still young enough to have another child, so who knows, I may fall in love tomorrow and start another family, anything is possible. It would have been a good story if I made it as a barrister, the stage that I am writing this book. I can picture myself in the wig and robe on the rear cover of this book, but as stated, there is nothing wrong with diverting one's goals. To make people aware of a story that doesn't involve constant success is a better message, as it is more realistic. More people will be able to relate to the story. Setting to many goals is wrong, I feel, as you become lazy. It is unrealistic for one to achieve success with multiple goals. I firmly believe that one must set two to three goals, which is all what is needed. This way you can work actively on achieving all of them. Failing is a good message to send out at times, as we should all be okay with failing. I have failed three areas of the bar course, but it has created a new direction for my energy. I am now more determined than ever to achieve my goals. It becomes a challenge for me to succeed, as I will not allow them to cheat me out of the bar course with the tech issues that were present, and instead I refocus and collect my thoughts by setting a new goal in another direction. It spurs me on when I fail, I must not ever allow a failure to beat me up. It is good to fail at times, as it allows you to cope with failure, it allows you to teach your body and mind to become more resilient. I kept my leg and that was the thanks to the fight in me, I am resilient. I have been taught the hard way, but thankful in many ways. The evenings I was homeless, lay in the field cold and wet, due to being turned away from my parents was a good learning curve. I became very resilient during them experiences and getting a mortgage at age twenty-one demonstrates such. I got up each morning, wet and cold, but still went looking for work. I was not going to allow my mum to destroy the man I am, it became a battle inside me that I must not allow her to win and instead fight back and succeed. It wasn't just the physical beatings, I had to battle in my mind as I grew into a man, as the verbal abuse was tougher for me to deal with. I was constantly told I would fail, and even during my degree my mum looked at me and said, 'you will not complete that degree, and you are wasting your time,' She frowned at me when saying this, I was always hurt by her verbal abuse. It was hard for me to get back up at times, but there is fire inside me and I will not go down for no one. That young Hillside kid was still lurking inside me, he would always pop up when a challenge was put before him. I recently attended my youngest sons' parents evening, as his mum allowed me to join her, instead of me arranging separate times. This was the first time it was allowed in eight years, which is nothing but sad, as it isn't about the parents. It is about the child and the need for the child to have parents who come together for them. There have been countless times where I have emailed requesting to join my son and his mum, but I have been ignored. It has got to the stage where today, I have no more fight in me when it comes to the want to co-parent. You can only take so much at times, and the fact is that my son is now old enough to do what he wants. My children are all doing well at school and university, they are happy, and healthy children, which is all what matters to me. There has been the odd time when I have not got on with the other parents at both of my son's football teams, as I am not part of the cliques that they have going on, not all the teams had this, but most. I am so very proud to come from Liverpool, as in Liverpool, we make everyone feel welcome, we don't form cliques and isolate people. You can walk up to any scouser and start chatting about your day and he will engage with you. People from some areas in Cheshire, not all, but some, are very different, they appear to form a clique during after school activities. I find anyone who forms a clique beyond pathetic and stuck up if anything. I laugh to myself, and I am glad to not be part of the clique. I don't want to associate myself with rude people. This is important for everyone; we must not want to join a group who are rude. Avoid people who stand around talking about others, especially when those others are present. These kinds of people always call others when they are with others, pretending to be tough, putting on an act or just being your typical busybody, but if you get them on their own, they soon quiet down. It was like a local lad, who was once mouthing off and threatening me in a Penketh pub for no reason what so ever. I took it all but later followed him to the chip shop away from the pub and his mates. I was prepared for a fight that night, but he backed down. He also stated in the pub that I was pretending to be on the phone when I wasn't. The day he referred to, which was many years before and totally irrelevant. I was on the phone that day, but the signal went, and I was unaware I had been cut off and I continued talking, not realising that the phone was down, that was all. I have nothing to prove to such people, and even my mates from Liverpool laughed and said for me to forget about the likes of them, as they are nothing to be concerned with. I was annoyed at myself that I didn't just ignore the incident at the pub and walk away, but it was around 2014, and my children were young. I couldn't take the chance on him approaching me when with my children. I needed to deal with that matter there and then, saying that I could have got into trouble with the police if fighting, and in turn ruining any chances I have of a career in law. Overall, the facts are that the correct thing to do, is to simply walk away and ignore such prats. I guess I was just dealing with a lot during that time and acted out of character by approaching him afterwards, as today I would very much just walk away and ignore such people, unless my children are about, as a parent naturally becomes protective in front of their children, I guess. The other facts are, and many youngsters need to be aware of this. No one ever wins an illegal fight. If you win and hurt the other person, you could go to prison, at the very least you will have a criminal record for assault, and that will affect you for a long time to come. It will also destroy any possibility you may have of wanting to enter certain careers. If you lose a fight, then yes, you may get badly hurt. The old school way is the better option, for me. Both meet up at the local boxing club and have it out in a safe environment, but overall, the best decision is to simply avoid such situations and walk away from them, when you can. People from Warrington are very different to the people who I grew up with around Hillside, Huyton. I am not calling all from Warrington / Cheshire, as they are mostly lovely people. It's like anywhere I guess; you just get a few idiots were ever you go. I find people are rude in most parts of the UK now, we seem to have lost some of that good old British welcoming personality. We should all treat people as they treat us, if they form a clique, then simply avoid such people. Most importantly, continuing being who you are, be nice, be happy and ignore any negative. Don't allow others to turn you into them. I keep myself to myself when I watch my son at football, he knows I love him, he knows I am watching and that is all what matters. My youngest son is very skilful, and this is due to the amount of time I spent with him at a young age. We would work on many football skills daily. It is hard for me watching my sons play football, as the standard of coaching at grassroots football is awful. You get these coaches screaming all kinds from the sidelines, it's embarrassing to watch. During my time at Stoke, I coached academy kids from a few clubs, this was after gaining 5 years grassroots experience. We would work on why they were let go from an academy and try to get them back in.

I also coached female football, and the girls I looked after played for some of the most well-known major southern clubs. I was also head coach of a female football team at a university. My coaching ability was of a high standard. You never heard me shouting all kinds from the sidelines, as I didn't need too. We worked on what was needed at training, and when it came to a match day, we put all our training into action. I was a good coach, and many would confirm that. I just find it annoying at times due to the terrible low standards that are present at grassroots today. I hear week in, week out, prats screaming, *'pass the ball'*, before the child even has the ball. It is meant to be enjoyment for the kids and nothing other. It certainly should not be causing panic to a child the second he gets the ball. This is not how you get the best out of any child. A parent during a match once said to me that the kids never seem to take a touch.

I agreed and repeated exactly what he said, but the coach turned around having a go at me, coming at me aggressively for no reason at all. He seemed envious of my coaching ability and knowledge. He only opened his mouth to me, as it was Infront of many others. One of those typical immature pathetic prats who mouth off when lots of people are around, but as stated, you get them on their own and they soon quiet down. I just ignore such people today and laugh to myself. I find it embarrassing how the odd few grown adult's act during kid's football. They should be setting an example, instead they are screaming, none stop, and most of what they scream doesn't even make sense.

The way I grew up in Liverpool, you would not mouth off or threaten people on the side line. Instead, you got a pair of gloves on at the local boxing club and had it out in the ring, shaking hands afterwards. This is what I experienced up to age 15. Shame adults can't be forced to do this, or bang heads together with the hope that they will simply grow up. I completely ignore it all and have done for a good while now, as my want for a career in law is far too important. I am very aware of my responsibility of having to set the correct example before my boys, and especially if one day representing the bar. I would like to finish off this chapter stating that I do feel that grassroots football could learn so very much from grassroots rugby' I have no real idea how rugby works, other than one must get the ball to the opposite end of the pitch. I popped along to a few local rugby matches. The first thing I observed was how mature the players behaved. They would bang into each other with such force and determination, yet two minutes later stand up and shake hands. The most impressive part was the standard of coaching.

The instructions sent onto the pitch made total sense, unlike most grassroots football these days. The parents all behaved well, too, and socialised afterwards. There was no aggression or immature behaviour at all. It is the total opposite to the behaviour you witness at some grassroots football these days, which is sad really, as I would have hoped that grassroots football would have progressed over the past 25 years since I started being part of it. Children are like a sponge, if they witness their own parents or aggressive silly coaches behaving badly. Then it is only setting one example, and it is the wrong one. Not all grassroots football is bad, as I have witnessed great levels of coaching in many areas, such as, in and around London, and many northern areas, such as Liverpool, Manchester etc. It is nice to know that there is also a lot out there who are setting the right example and making football nothing other than enjoyable for the kids, whether they win or lose!

Chapter Twenty

The Lost Son

The story of the Lost Son is very relevant to me and my family, I feel, there are many comparisons. I have made so many mistakes but repaired myself and become a good man. I have worked so hard in liking me as a man and father. I am proud of who I am and proud of what I have achieved, but I still often look back and wish I could turn back the clock at times. I am aware that mistakes make us who we are today, and I like me today. I just would have liked to have repaired some areas of my life and avoided certain matters, especially matters that involved my divorce, as it would have benefited my children to have avoided certain situations when going through my divorce. The story of Jacob is also relevant to my family, especially during my fathers passing. It's like a mirror image in part. Ironically, I got The Battle of Jacob tattooed on my lower left ribs. I liked the story for other reasons and was unaware of the relevance with my family until recently. I now find it very ironic how I got that tattoo, and with how the story was drawn to me in the first instance. I fell asleep whilst reading my bible and dreamt of the issues surrounding my mum and brother, with how they acted during my father's passing, and with how they have deceived me and my sister since. I woke up and the bible fell to the floor, opening the pages in the process, and revealing The Battle of Jacob. I only read a few verses and decided on getting a tattoo. It was only a year later after getting the tattoo that I decided to read the full story, and I was shocked how much it resembled the situation that surrounded my father's passing. I sometimes wish I could turn back the clock to a certain event or day. One day that springs to mind is the five pence bus ride. I was living at Bruton Road at the time, I would have been approximately seven. Me and my friend, Lee, decided to go on a bus ride. We paid five pence and ended up in Liverpool city centre, which wasn't bad since we got the bus from the bottom of Hillside Ave, Huyton. We were two very young kids let loose in the city, and full of energy. We made our way to Mount Pleasant, which back then had a cinema. We paid to watch a movie. I still have no idea how we would have had money on us at the time to afford the cinema. We caused all kinds of trouble that day, and I can still remember a lot of it. I loved going to the cinema, I mostly went alone. When we moved to Warrington, as stated, I hated it and would look at any excuse to go back to Liverpool. If ever I needed to buy trainers, I would get the bus back to Liverpool and go directly to St Johns Market, as that is where my auntie took me as a child. I would walk to the bubble bus stops, and stand waiting, but as I waited, I would look across at the Cannon cinema and always end up walking across to watch whatever movie was due to start next. I watched, Ghost, this was the day I fell in love with Demi Moore. I remember hearing people crying during this movie. I also remember watching, Mannequin, and I absolutely loved it, and still watch it repeatedly today. The cinema was my escape from reality, it was my escape from the abuse. It allowed me to have only happy thoughts, and I would always leave the cinema on a high, am sure we all feel the same when it comes to the cinema experience. It is a magical experience at times when visiting the cinema. The cinema can be relevant to every part of life, be it happy or sad. The experience can give you fresh hope and even make you feel motivated in setting new goals and challenges. I have a watched a few children's movies recently, and they can be a reminder that the world is different through the eyes of a child. I have highlighted much abuse I suffered as a child, and at times it may have been on a scale of six or seven looking back, but at the time it was scale of ten. My point is that some situations you may feel are minor, but to a child they may be viewed as very serious. We all must be aware of this, and this is why it is so important to not talk adult matters in front of a child. I look back at my own divorce, and when finding out about an affair, I hate myself for allowing my emotions get the better of me, and allowing my children hear me bad mouth their mother. I was just in shock and panicking that I was losing my family was all. We are only human, and we all react negatively at times, sadly. Saying all that we all have a duty to protect our children from hearing anything negative between parents, as it is abuse and it can affect a child's mind. My mum would always put me down, saying negative words, and at that time am sure she thought nothing of it, but I have carried those abusive words with me all my life. When I lost my father, I visited my sister's home a few weeks later. My mother called my sister, and I had to listen to my mum bad mouth me, saying terrible things about me for no reason whatsoever. I am a son that she can be proud of, but for some reason she is full of hate towards me. My sister stuck up for me that day, just as I would always stick up for her. I will never allow my mum to say a bad word about my sister or her family again. I have no idea how any parent could be nasty to a child of their own. Am aware it was different back in the day, but it still doesn't make sense. My grandparents were loving parents, amazing people, so there is no reason for my mum to turn out full of hatred. I often look back and wonder why I was disliked so much. Yes, I was trouble at times, but not that bad. I never took drugs or hurt anyone. It was mostly harmless trouble that I created, but always taken seriously. When we moved to Penketh, I got several jobs that meant me having to peddle to work. I got a job working nights at Whithouse Industrial Estate. It was just over seven miles from the house, which meant I had to leave a couple of hours beforehand to get there on time. I would finish work at 6.30 a.m. and would have to peddle all that way home in the cold. I had this job for six months before getting a new role as a security guard, which also meant peddling for hours. It makes me proud of my son seeing him go to work today of an evening and coming home at 8 a.m. It takes me back to the days I did the same at his age. I still feel bad towards myself, as I feel I should be offering more, so he doesn't have to work those hours, but on a positive note. It will do him good, keeping him fit and healthy, as he is constantly on the go, which is only a good thing.

I can't escape looking at myself today, feeling that I have failed in so many ways. It is hard to escape those feelings, and they do get the better of me at times, and I can become emotional. This is a good lesson for the young, as stated, time is so very valuable, and it cannot be wasted. I also feel that mistakes should be avoided, as a lot of mistakes you can end up carrying with you well into adulthood. We make mistakes and think it's nothing, but sometimes those mistakes are bigger than we realise, and we always seem to realise when it is too late. I do feel school is a perfect example, as so many youngsters go to school thinking it is of no real importance. If only they knew just how important it is, not just academically, but also in learning how to deal with real life situations, such as bullying, relationships, and dishonesty, the list is endless, and that is why I disagree with home schooling. Home schooling, I feel, will only allow for a child to miss out on so many valuable life lessons.

I have had my fair share of lessons, the one lesson that hit me hard was having to go to prison for six weeks. I was seventeen years old at the time, I remember it all very well. I was first banned from driving for drink driving. I had only been out of the army for a matter of a few months and was offered work by my next-door neighbour as a labourer. He managed to get work at an army base in South Wales. I went along, and it was all exciting at first, but during our first weekend it all went wrong. We were in a nightclub where mostly soldiers visited. I was drinking 20/20. It was a lethal drink that would get you drunk at speed. I started arguing with a doorman and cannot remember why. My neighbour intervened, pulling me away, but I ended up throwing a punch towards him. I left the club and began walking back to the caravan. I got back and found the keys to the pickup. I wanted to go home, so I got in the pickup and began driving. I drove straight into another caravan when a male came out shouting. I drove on to a country lane, and put the windows down, so I could try to sober up. A police car pulled up beside me, telling me to pull over. I refused at first. Eventually I pulled up and I was given a good kicking by the officers, who clearly disliked that I had a scouse accent. That doesn't go down well in South Wales, especially if drink driving. I was taken back to the station and several months later I had to attend court. A friend from Penketh drove me to the court where I was handed a two-year ban and large fine. A local police officer came to my parents' home to collect my driving license. It was disgusting behaviour from me, and being drunk is no excuse. I could have killed myself, or even worse, I could have hurt someone else. I behaved better in the coming months, and kept my head down, but one night whilst I was on a night out at Warrington, I met a much older female at Mr Smith's night club. I ended up going back to a house that was a shelter for battered up wives. She was around thirty-five at the time and I didn't think much of it all. It was exciting going with a much older woman. I started to date her, and she would pick me up in her car. She made me aware that she had suffered domestic abuse in the hands of her partner, who she had children with too. She was in the house to escape him and appeared to live in fear. She told me that on several occasions she had tried to kill herself. I felt sorry for her, but at that age, I couldn't offer her any real help. The female called me one morning telling me that she may be pregnant. I didn't know what to say but asked if I could meet her. She picked me up in her mini metro, and we went for a drive. Whilst driving she began panicking slightly, so I drove for her. A police car pulled up behind us with blue lights flashing, I jumped into the rear seat with the kids, and my girlfriend grabbed the steering wheel. The officer told me to get out, as it was obvious I was driving. I was taken back to Huyton police station and put before the Magistrates court. I was handed a six-week prison sentence. I remember being in a security van, where I sat in a small cubicle. I was allowed to call my parents and make them aware, but my uncle answered my dad's shop phone, and he was laughing and made my dad aware what had happened. I remember arriving at prison where I was strip searched. There were another two males sitting with me and it was their first time at prison too. One of them was handed six weeks like me, but the other handed 12 months. They had an argument with a chip shop owner over an order, so they got a pellet gun and began firing pellets into the shop. The male in the passenger seat who didn't fire anything was handed six weeks for going along with the other male. I could see that they were both in fear, I was feeling okay, as I had experienced far worse when locked up in army cells. I was taken to my own cell, where I immediately began cleaning and making the bed. My first inspection involved the main prison officer visiting my cell. He asked me if I had been in the army, and I replied with a 'yes'. He told me it was obvious due to how clean and tidy my cell was. I started to dislike the prison at speed, due to the other prisoners. I would draw pictures of the outside world on tissue paper and stick it to my wall. They were pictures of the view I had from my cell window. I started to play pool against other prisoners and became friends with a few. I recognised a few prisoners from Hillside Avenue, who also recognised me. One afternoon, prisoners with orange suits walked in, they looked like serious offenders. One of them approached me, he was a huge guy. He asked me if I knew a female, and I replied it was my auntie. He knew who I was and told me that if I have any issues to go to him. He was classed as a dangerous prisoner, as he had escaped the previous prison. They raised a forklift truck in the prison yard, where building work was taking place and they climbed over the wall and got away before getting caught in Wales. There was also a stabbing in the prison during my time there, which made the experience a lot scarier. I was visited by my uncle, and my parents. My uncle had been in prison, so he offered me advice. I took all on board but was still left with some fear. I was finally released and swore that I would never return to such a place. I have not committed any offences since then that was wholly my fault. I cannot blame myself for the breaches of the court orders relating to my family court matters, as stated, it was clear that I was badly treated. I always refer to the advice I have been given, If we are hanging out with the wrong crowd, or hanging out with anyone negative, then it is only ever going to attract negative towards us. I never saw that female since I was arrested, but my parents did state that she came into the shop asking for me. I often thought and wonder if she was pregnant and wonder if she had the baby, I don't think she did, but many years later whilst I was married and had my two eldest children in the car, who were approximately six at the time, I saw the female crossing the road and my wife at the time asked me if I knew that person due to how I looked at her. I replied, 'yes, and I wonder if that girl with her, was my daughter.' I explained the story to my wife, who stated that she would accept anyone if they turned up stating that I am their father. I should have got out the car that day and spoke to her, but I didn't. This isn't the first time where I thought I may have a child, as in November 2021 I got a female pregnant who lived at Tamworth. We had only been dating for nine weeks when she got the pregnancy test out and showed me it. She appeared very excited about it all and informed me that she had an illness that prevents pregnancy. I heard her on the phone to her mum and they both appeared very excited. She stated that when a woman is pregnant, they produce a hormone, and the hormone can clear the illness she suffered from. We split up a few weeks later, and she informed me that she had an abortion. She blocked me on Facebook, but I set up another Facebook account, as I had to be sure that she didn't have the baby. I looked at the females Facebook, but to my shock she closed her Facebook down within two weeks of us splitting up. I have never seen her since, and often think if she had the baby, but again, I don't think she did. My life has constantly had drama in it, and I have mostly wondered about feeling lost. I am the Lost Son in a way, but the positive is that I have learnt the right way. The negative is that I have learnt far too late and due to that I missed out on so many opportunities. I often look at the calendar and turn each page reminding myself that is a whole month gone again, so much can be achieved in a single month. I always have several calendars now, as it is a reminder that time is limited. It is my way of keeping a close eye on my activities and making sure I am doing as much as I can with my time. I don't think I will ever get over how much time I have wasted through the years. I will never forgive myself for all the wrongs I have done. The only way I can apologise for the wrongs, is for me to become a perfect man and father. I want to give and help as much as I can, I remind myself that I have never bullied anyone, or physically hurt anyone. I have never taken drugs or committed a fraudulent act, but this doesn't mean that I have not committed a wrongful act. Committing criminal damage to a tractor I drove when I was young upset my father, and he went through a lot back then due to my behaviour. I can see how I put my parents through a lot but beating me didn't help in any way. It only made matters worse and affected my mental state of mind. Today I am constantly pulled up by my two sons, they make me aware when I act childish or wrong in any way. I must accept that the Hillside lad in me will always lurk in some way. I must make sure that when he pops out, he pops out in a way that cannot get me into trouble. Don't get me wrong here, I don't mean that young lad pops out of me in a violent way. He just pops out when wrong is committed against me, It is how I react that lets me down at times. I do not allow wrong against me, and I always stick up for what is right, but there are ways of going about it all. I am very quick to write a formal complaint when wrong is done. This may appear to be okay and correct, but you must ask yourself, what energy are you using up, how is it effecting your mood and personality. It is good to turn a cheek at times, even when wrong is committed against you, as you don't waste energy. You always stay positive and in a good frame of mind, so there are many advantages to letting things go at times. I am so proud of my boys, as there have been times where I want to complain about a bad service or a wrong against me. My boys speak up and say to me to just let it go. I am an extremely proud father, I know what is right and wrong, as I have committed so many wrongs, but I have also done a lot of good.

I am aware which road is more rewarding, sadly it took me forty years to realise it all. I am thankful that my boys have learnt it all quickly, and I am confident that they will grow in to fine gentlemen, who will one day be perfect partners and fathers. I know that my father looks down with pride, he loved my kids very much. He loved all his grandchildren equally. I know he loved me too; I am just struggling still with how I was treated differently. It will take me many years to get over it all. It is a healing process, I guess, and this book has been a good way of getting rid of some of the baggage that I carry on my shoulders. I have been able to release it all, it is as though I have shouted from the rooftop, and it has finally left my system.

Chapter Twenty-One

Which way now

I will always look back over my life and feel that most of it was a failure, but at the same time, I have a lot to be proud of. I have achieved academically and continue to achieve, and on route towards my PHD. I have a long way to go yet, but I am getting there. My story doesn't smell of roses, and at times it's frustrating, disappointing, and sad, but one thing is for sure, my story has lots of content. I have never had a dull moment, there has always been excitement in some way. My actions in life have gone against all the wise words of advice that I have received, that being that all the correct things in life are boring. I have, sadly, always done the opposite to boring. It is hard to know that my eldest son at just age nineteen earns more than his dad, but at the same time it makes me proud of me, knowing that I work hard, leaving myself with nothing to make sure he has a roof over his head. I don't take any keep from him and make sure he has nice presents at birthdays and Christmas. I don't want much now, I still have my goal of a power boat and caravan, but that is it really. I have made the home a lovely one, and that is in the children's best interests. I have created a good inheritance for them one day and it settles my mind knowing I will leave a lot to them after I am gone. A good man and father will never be too concerned with what he has for himself, as he is only concerned with how he provides for others. I have never not provided, and always given all I can, when I can. I was upset with child maintenance contacting me one time, and taking £1,000 too much, in the way of an over payment from my wages. I made sure that they didn't get another penny, but I also made sure that I kept giving as much as I could, and more than what was ever asked for by Child Maintenance. They were never needed in our lives due to the fact I was always providing anyway. I have never claimed working tax credits or child support. My ex-wife has always claimed it all, even when we were together, she claimed without me knowing. I have never asked for any of it, as it is for the children. I just make sure that they have all they want and need. I am very aware that my ex-wife also works hard and provides a lot for them too. My children have good parents who love them very much. Not all kids these days have good parents and for a whole range of different reasons. The world has gone mad in so many ways, people identifying mental illness as just another way of behaving is a good example. My children have traditional parents, and although we have our many differences, we both believe in hard work, paying bills, doing well academically, and providing holidays when we can, and that's it in a nutshell. The best way of living life is a simple life, I have registered for my second master's degree that was meant to start next year, but yesterday I was forced to move it to the summer of next year for financial reasons, as the cost of the course is a lot. Kids have no idea how good they have it, and sadly, a lot are not reminded what is on offer for them. I have the idea of approaching a few schools and requesting that I give a talk. I want to make kids aware of the importance of time, and that they must do well at school. I want to make them aware how much fun college is and university. I want to make them aware how much of it is for free, and where there are costs, a student loan is available, that is only to be paid back in small portions. There are so many options for the young today. It is wrong that so many schools are not reminding the children constantly of what is on offer for them if they do well at school. There are good schools out there and good teachers, I am aware of this. There is good and bad everywhere, and in every organisation. The days of us having to fight to find out what is on offer are long gone. There are so many departments' youngsters can now approach. There are also lots of charities out there that offer good advice. If a child suffers in any way, they cannot be discriminated against, and they must be treated equally. I wanted my book to be written in a particular style, I didn't want it to be written as though an experienced professor has written it. I wanted it in the style of a Hillside kid who got himself out of the Unit for badly behaved kids, got himself out of prison, and went on to complete a law degree and much more, setting a great example to his own children and others. I think I have successfully achieved what I set out to do. I hope that my story is a message to others, especially to the ones who are hanging out with the wrong crowd, or who are messing about in school. It doesn't get you anywhere, and I beg any youngster who reads my book to believe me. Time is priceless, it must be cherished and spent wisely. Do not get to my age and decide to study like I did, instead please, start doing it now, start making your life better now. Start wanting to like yourself and start wanting to improve as a person. I often tell my son that the hard work he is doing now, may not be a benefit right now, but later in life he will be thankful he worked hard, as he will have so many more doors open for him as an adult. That's all what it's about for me, how many doors can you open, or how many keys can you collect to open doors.

'As an example, If you achieve a degree, it will open a few more job opportunities. Look at this as opening doors, look at this as gaining a few more keys. If you complete a course as an Electrician, you open many doors as a job being an electrician. The more you achieve academically, the more doors you will have available to you. If you leave school with nothing, yes you may get a job, and it may be a good one, but the facts are, you will have less doors available to you.'

I am sick of reading quotes that highlight a degree doesn't make you more intelligent. No one has ever stated that it does, but it does make you more intelligent in the subject you specialised in. It also demonstrates you can research and have a learning ability. It demonstrates you can read and take in what you read, so a degree holds much weight. Youngsters need to realise that the prats who create these statements are jealous people who I assume didn't achieve academically, so they now go to war with the world of academics. If my message can hit home with just one youngster, then I have done what I set out to do with this book. I hear so many stories on certain TV programmes, or in the media, with how a billionaire started off with nothing, how he had no education and became super rich. This also sends out the wrong message, as youngsters then feel that they can achieve all with no academic achievements. My father once told me that if he started his grocery business in the year 2000 onwards, he would never have become successful and probably gone bust after a few years. This is due to the amount of large supermarket express stores that are now in existence. He was right too; it would be impossible for him to create the same success he did if he started today. My point is that the world changes constantly, and societies with it. The billionaire who became a billionaire lived in a very different world that it is today. There are far less opportunities today than what there were many years ago. The internet is a good example, every idea is taken up almost. Yes, there are still many millionaires in the UK, and in fact, just over 4% are millionaires, but the population of the UK is near sixty-seven million and growing daily. The odds of becoming rich are not great, especially in a country that is growing at speed. I won't get into how I find that frustrating, with how the way the country is growing far too fast and causing the likes of the NHS to fail at times and creating a housing crisis. My point is, you need to open as many doors as you can, and the other fact is that you must go to school, so whilst there you may as well make the most of it. You may even have a bad experience at times during school, college or university. I know I did, but don't allow some idiot pupil, teacher or tutor ruin your chances of academic success. The best way to win is to not engage with anything negative. If a teacher dislikes you, then don't allow that prat to win by you becoming a loser. Instead, get your head down and succeed. The day you leave with positive results, smile at the teacher, and say to yourself, 'I won'. The issue I had growing up, was that the Hillside lad would take over in me, and resort to a negative response that would only make matters worse for me. We must not allow others to make us who we are. They don't have a remote control for us, and we shouldn't respond as though we are a dog being trained. Never react to other people's actions, and instead stay calm and think about your next move. Think how it will affect you and think how you can get out of the situation and into a winning position. I could sit around hating the world and many people in it with how I have been treated badly, but I don't. I remind myself that it is their issue that they did me wrong. I remind myself that I must continue to stay on track and strive to become better each day. I will not ever again allow others make me who I am, and I will not allow them to make me react to their wrongful behaviour. I will stay being who I am, as I like me, and I am not changing for no one. I will always offer my ex-wife help and she knows I am here if she ever needs me. I do get upset that no one visited me in hospital recently, and often look back at the time I didn't see my kids, or how the police spoke to my daughter about a loving WhatsApp message I sent to her, making her aware I sent money, but I can't allow them situations control my life moving forwards. I also don't want to meet my next partner on a negative, where I constantly speak about the past and past negative experiences. So many people meet each other and instantly begin to talk negatively about their ex-partner or previous life. It instantly paints a negative picture, a dark cloud above you. I instead plan to only speak how I am, proud how well my children are doing and instead speak positively. How you feel on the inside is who you are on the outside. If you are constantly thinking negative thoughts, you become ugly on the outside. I firmly believe this, it also affects one's health, as you are constantly tense. Happy thoughts create happy feelings, it is like going for a run or popping to the gym. You exercise having only positive thoughts and it helps your performance. I train myself daily to never react to others, yes, at times I fail, but I am failing less and less as the days go by. I react less to other people who commit road rage. Instead, I turn the music volume up and smile to myself and continue with my journey. The other person is left angry and frustrated that they didn't get a reaction. They will be wound up all day, this isn't great for their health. The sad fact is, we live in an ugly world today, a world full of anger and hatred. The good old days of smiles and walking every few yards to a good morning or good afternoon are long gone. I firmly believe it is due to so many traditions being taken from us. Christmas is such a happy time, it is a time of loving and giving, yet so many in the UK now want to tone it down. There are less signs that state 'Christmas', instead the powers that be are wanting to name it, 'The Holidays'. There are less decorations and lights, why would anyone want to tone down happy times. Easter is the same, it is being toned down, I feel. If you look back at the video footage of the 70s/80s these festive seasons were celebrated with so much happiness, and happiness is only a good thing that should only ever be encouraged. We can't live paying attention too much to the outside world, as you will never change what is going on. You will only ever bring yourself frustration. My grandmother banned my granddad from watching the news once and it worked, he moaned less and spoke positively more often. You can offer your little bit to the world becoming a better place by walking outside with a smile. If you smile at someone they will always smile back. It is like a cough, ever notice how one coughs in an office and then suddenly there are many coughs. If you start laughing for no reason whatsoever, the person in front of you will start laughing too. We need more laughing and smiling in this world, and that will only happen if we all leave the house smiling. People often smile more when they feel good about themselves. I have found myself liking who I am more and more. I have noticed I am smiling more often because of it. My father always said you should never disrespect a working man. I am working, and although I earn very little, I am still working and that carries some respect, which makes me happy. It makes me feel good about who I am as a man. So many people feel bad about who they are and the last thing we need is others making us feel worse, but sadly, so many people make others feel worse and don't seem bothered by it. There are so many in society who have no self-awareness. Tutors at university can come across as snobbish, and unhelpful, not realising that students are customers, we are consumers who have paid for a service that we have a right to receive. I am still disappointed in the experience I had during the weekend residential stay, and with how a few of the KC's behaved in a snobbish manner. I feel that snobs live in a bubble, a bubble where they only ever see each other. When they venture outside, they are put off by what they see, as they think that they are better than it all. They move from their circle of friends and feel awkward speaking to others, they finally move away and go back to join their own kind. Thankfully not all KC's or barristers are like this, as most are approachable and lovely people, so too Judges. It is like anywhere in life, you will always come across a few snobs, snobs who think they are better. Where now, for me, I find life boring most of the time. I often sit staring at the clock and wonder when it is bedtime. I can then get cosy in bed and watch a movie. I always seem to get a good night's sleep, and I go to sleep feeling positive, as I make sure each day is productive in some way, even if it is writing a few thousand words. It keeps my mind feeling positive. I always make sure I have plans for the coming months, even if it is only a weekend trip away, It is still a plan. Creating memories is all what matters for me now, I must create as many happy memories as possible for my children and hopefully we have our powerboat soon enough and maybe a caravan. This will allow us to pop away to Wales every few weeks as a family. I remind myself that most of the bills are up to date and that's all-what matters. I am also aware that whilst I am working, I can apply for better and more suitable roles, and I am doing just that. I know that if I get to the stage of my PHD and if I complete it, I will have achieved my main goal in life. I can one day teach maybe, or write more books, even about law, who knows what will become possible. I want to give talks and feel that my story allows me to do that. I can make youngsters aware of the dangers of wasting time, or the dangers of entering the wrong road. I know what it is like to be disliked for behaving badly,

I also know what it is like to feel negative about yourself. The message in my story is a positive one, anyone can achieve within reason. I do feel it of importance to always be realistic, don't set your goals to high, as otherwise you fail, and you're left feeling deflated and negative. Setting easy achievable targets is the way to go. This way you hit every goal, gradually making the goals more intense, but as you hit each goal you start to feel more and more positive, and your motivation grows, you start to grow and start feeling better about yourself. My goal at first was to only do well at college, which I achieved. I wanted to then complete another small goal, which was a completion of a four-week criminology course, this was a little taste of studying criminology. I achieved this, so I went on and created a slightly tougher target, this being a six-week fast track to university. I didn't think that this would be possible, but I completed the course. I made it to university and that was enough for me, as I didn't dream that I would be able to complete a degree, but I did, so I continued to set other goals, but always making sure that each goal was easy enough for me to achieve it. I never created goals that was out of reach. My dad always said for me to write a goal and put it on the wall, and I did just that. I would wake up each morning looking at the goal. I could clearly place myself in the picture. It was picture of me standing in a court room representing a client, but as stated, it is perfectly okay to change your picture and make a new goal. There are no set rules, and you are always in control of your own life. It is you who sets the pace and makes the rules. You must believe in yourself, and always remember that, if you have a roof over your head, and that you are happy, and healthy, then nothing else matters. You can choose to do very little with your life if you wish, if doesn't make you worse than anyone else. It is others who are a prisoner in their own life who feel that they must do certain things to be accepted.

I always say to not take advice from the rich, as most of the rich were just in the right place at the right time, or they were born with a silver spoon in their mouths. I also say to not listen to Hollywood actors who behave like they know it all, when they know very little. In my book, anyone can act, and most actors today are ex sportspeople or ex gangsters off the street. Anyone can act and they are no one special, they act for a living, most have been in the right place at the right time. They live in multi-million-pound homes. Yet look down giving advice to the ordinary man. The best people to take advice from, is always the closest people around you. Listen to people who have been where you are now, and who understand what it is like, as they have lived the life you are living right now. I have lived the life of a naughty school kid, I have lived the life of a victim who was badly shot, and someone who went through an emotional divorce process, I have also been homeless and suffered abuse. I can relate to so many who suffer. Today, all I want to do is to help others, offering support when I can. I am wanting to volunteer as a child mentor and do more within the community. This will keep me occupied and it clears my mind, it allows me to pray knowing that I am helping others, and that I am growing as a man. I am aware I will always suffer some form of trauma, as I still sit in a certain position when visiting a pub. The PTSD is locked away at the back of my mind, but my body remembers the trauma from time to time. I will still watch a movie and relate to what is happening, especially if it involves shooting incidents or PTSD. At times I flinch for no reason, also, just before going to sleep, I get a shock, it's like something has hit me. I jump, get out of bed, and check the window. I have no idea why I do this, I do it whilst driving long distances as well. I flinch as though there is a gun pointing at me and it's getting ready to fire. It's a horrible thing and hopefully I will be completely cured of it one day. I must continue to respond correctly, not ever allowing my past to get the better of me or affecting who I am today. I have come too far and worked far too hard for it to all go to waste. We all carry wounds in some way, but we can use those experiences to help others who may have experienced similar. I continue to pray and often speak to my father and grandmother throughout the day; I remind them that I am becoming a better man, and that I am aware that my children look at me as an example. I have grown, becoming a good man and father. I don't want to ever forget my roots, as I want to be proud that I am from Hillside. I want to be proud that I came from the schools I attended. One must never be ashamed of where they came from, as it is who they are. The people who still live in those areas are just as good as you, they are the same and you are no better. No number of degrees or any amount of money makes you better than others. It is who you are as a man, and how you react. Whilst on this subject it is important for me to highlight that you will struggle to find a town in the world that has produced more actors, playwriters, sportspeople and much more that what Huyton has. I am proud to be a Huyton lad. My chess continues to help me in many ways, as it keeps me focused. I am proud that my chess started in Kensington Library, and going back to this original club has been the best decision I have made for my chess, as it has engulfed my passion for chess once more. Chess will always play a role in my life, once chess is in you, it never leaves. It really is like life, it allows you to analyse your moves before making them, we all should do this in life. We all react far too much at times when it can be so easily avoided. I once saw the Royal Family on TV. There were people screaming abuse from the roadside during the event. Prince Charles, who is now King, didn't turn to look at the people who shouted the abuse. He instead ignored it all, as though those people were not there. It was as though they didn't exist. He was blind and deaf to them, as he knew he was above those bad people. The thugs hurtling terrible abuse were so below him, he didn't see them. He continued to smile and refused to allow those people change who he is and how he reacted to the nice people. This was a good lesson in how to react to negative people. I have tried to grow as much as possible and I have a long way to go still, but I am getting there. The good people of Liverpool have one thing in common, that is that they don't give up. They are always ready to fight for what is right and there are many examples, Hillsborough is one example. I am very proud to come from Merseyside. I will always strive to become the best version of me and continue to improve as a man. I am also ready to battle if it is needed, as it is important to fight for what is right, if it makes sense to enter such a battle that is. My last message in this book is to my dad, who once said, 'You will never become a barrister.' Dad, maybe I won't become a barrister, and that is perfectly okay. I have become a good man and a father who sets the correct example, and that is all what matters. I have achieved in life, and I will continue to achieve. I will achieve my main aim in life, in completing my PHD, and that is a fact. One day, if I am asked about my book, anyone can ask me, 'Did you complete your PHD?' I will say, 'YES', as the Hillside kid in me doesn't allow me to give up. I may have also achieved my other goal, with being called to the bar, who knows.

''He was lost and is found.'

Luke 15:24

* 9 7 8 1 0 6 8 5 3 5 9 0 1 *